CW01545579

Modes of Sentience

Peter Sjöstedt-Hughes

Published by
Psychedelic Press
London, UK

Modes of Sentience: Psychedelics, Metaphysics, Panpsychism
Copyright © 2021
Peter Sjöstedt-Hughes and Psychedelic Press

ISBN: 9781916266735

All rights reserved. This work can only be reproduced with written permission by the author or publisher, except passages for reasons of review.

Moth mezzotints (of the Common Quaker and White Ermine) on covers by Sarah Gillespie: www.sarahgillespie.co.uk – ©Sarah Gillespie 2021

Design and typesetting by Peter Sjöstedt-Hughes

For more information:
www.psychedelicpress.co.uk
www.philosopher.eu

Dedicated to my late father, artist Don Hughes

Contents

Acknowledgements
Preface   i

I.   **Panpsychism**:   1
      Ubiquitous Sentience

II.   **Conspectus of A. N. Whitehead's Metaphysics**   23

III. **The Concrescence of Dissent**:   29
      Whitehead as Religious, Scientific, Philosophic Heretic

IV.   **Psychedelic Experience**:   57
      Revelation, Hallucination, or Otherwise?

V.   **The Psychedelic Influence on Philosophy**   65

VI.   **Substance and Process**: An Outline   87

VII. **The Great God Pan is Not Dead**: Alfred North   99
      Whitehead and the Psychedelic Mode of Perception

VIII. **The Pentalogy of Perception**   117

IX.   **The First Scientific Psychonaut**:   129
      Sir Humphry Davy

X.   **Deeper than Depth**:   155
      N-Dimensional Space and Sentience

Chapter Sources   187
Reference List   191

Acknowledgements

This book would not be possible without the help, writings, and/or conversations with a number of people, so I give my deepest thanks to the following. Robert Dickins for his thoughtful editing of this volume, for his conversation and good friendship. Also in the Psychedelic Press group I thank Nikki Wyrd, Rosalind Stone, and Julian Vayne. For my doctoral thesis that runs parallel to, yet crosses, this volume, I thank Michael Hauskeller, Tom Roberts, and John Dupré, as well as Joel Krueger and Galen Strawson, who both examined and passed my thesis. I also thank Galen for 'peer-reviewing' the first chapter in this book. I heartily give thanks to Prof. Christine Hauskeller who has acted as a fantastic mentor to my postdoctorate research fellowship, and for being a good friend. I must also thank Elizabeth and Lenny Gibson for supporting my work in many ways, for which I can never give enough gratitude. Likewise must I thank John Buchanan for his extraordinary trust, support, and friendship. I also thank the people at TEDx Truro who enabled my talk there on 'Psychedelics and Consciousness', especially Donna Black. For the mezzotint moths that adorn the covers I thank artist Sarah Gillespie (www.sarahgillespie.co.uk) for her permission of use. I could not have created any writing without the love and support of my mother Kattis Sjöstedt-Hughes, my late father Don Hughes, my brother Ted, my brother Paul and his family – and my endearing wife Anja for her constant support, tolerance, and love, and my two marvellous little children, my sweet Arthur and Isolde.

Preface

The moth was named *Psyche* by Aristotle, a term that also referred to the soul, the mind, the breath, and to the winged goddess who travelled to the underworld and back, metamorphizing from mere mortal to eternal deity. This myth is quite the *psyche*delic trip itself, and thus doth the moth open and close on the covers of this book.

What is it like to be a moth, attracted both to the night and to the light? What modes of sentience exist in our world unfathomable to the normal human modes of sentience? That there are modes, modifications, or types of sentience pertaining to a vast array of distinct types of beings is a ramification of the panpsychism set out in chapters of this volume. Sentience here is not rare but floods reality. Human sentience too has many modes in ordinary living, yet many more still experienced in the psychedelic state – states of extraordinary being.

The term *Modes of Sentience* that titles this collection of essays refers then to both panpsychism and psychedelic phenomenology – to types of *beings* and to types of *being*. But I also use the term due to its connotations to Benedict de Spinoza and Alfred North Whitehead. Spinoza, following an Aristotelian-Cartesian tradition, uses the term 'mode' to refer to tokens of space and sentience, both of which are 'attributes' (expressions) of the one 'substance' that he calls *God or Nature*. The title echoes too Whitehead's late tome, *Modes of Thought*, which is a book I always recommend enquirers to begin with when approaching Whitehead, both for its clarity and its wide ambit.

As with my previous volume, *Noumenautics*, I apologize for any repetition found in this book – a flaw that can only defend itself by claiming that it makes each chapter independently intelligible. Though there is an order to the chapters, they need not necessarily be read in linear fashion.

The texts in the following pages were written for the most during my PhD (on 'Pansentient Monism'). In fact, some of that doctoral thesis can be found within these pages. Just as there are various modes of sentience, so are there various levels of complexity pertaining to each chapter. Some are easy to read, others require more effort. These essays concern varieties of conscious to subconscious sentience, or mind, in ways phenomenological, epistemic, noetic, and geometric: we end with a trip into the underworld depths where sentience intersects with n-dimensional space: a space not limited to three dimensions. We here take flight down through altered states of space, time, mind, matter, and all that lies within.

Peter Sjöstedt-Hughes
West Penwith, Cornwall
November 2021

I

Panpsychism
Ubiquitous Sentience

We must learn to understand nature from ourselves, not ourselves from nature.[1]
– Schopenhauer

The word *panpsychism* is a Renaissance compound[2] of the Ancient Greek *pan* (all) and *psyche* (mind, or soul). It is thus the doctrine that minds[3] exist fundamentally[4] throughout all of actuality[5] – from humans, hawks, honeybees and trees, down to bacteria, mycelia, molecules, and the subatomic below these. All of matter includes minds. Panpsychism is, in itself, a secular doctrine unlike *pantheism* (that Nature is God) and unlike *animism*[6] (that rivers and winds, etc., each have a spirit). It is generally unlike *idealism* in that it takes matter to be real[7] rather than ideal (as mere projection of the mind); it is generally unlike *dualism* in that it does not take mind to be separate from matter, but rather takes mind to be intrinsic to matter;[8] and it is unlike *physicalism* as understood to imply that most matter be insentient.[9]

Panpsychism differentiates within the suffix *psyche* a vast variety of states of sentience, and it mostly attributes sentience to quasi-autopoietic (self-systematic) entities such as organisms and molecules, rather than to aggregates thereof, such as rocks and radiators. In the hierarchy of states of mind, 'consciousness' is an uncommon complex crown of sentience. All has mind though not all has consciousness, let alone self-consciousness. Even Plato acknowledged such distinctions, stating that, '[t]he plant ... is without belief or reason or understanding but has appetite and a sense of pleasure and pain.'[10]

As it stands, panpsychism bears a proud history of eminent thinkers from the very beginnings of Western philosophy via thinkers such as Thales and Heraclitus, through to great Renaissance figures such as Patrizi (who coined the term *panpsychism*) and Bruno, to the mind-matter cognoscenti of the modern era: Spinoza, Leibniz, Schopenhauer, William James, A. N. Whitehead, and arguably Bertrand Russell to name but a small number.[11] The last few decades have brought a renewed interest and advocacy for the theory from the likes of Thomas Nagel, David Chalmers, and, most influentially, from Galen Strawson.

It was Chalmers who renamed the mind-body, or mind-matter problem as the 'hard problem of consciousness',[12] and it is perhaps the renewed interest in this problem that has fueled re-interrogation of panpsychism as its solution. The mind-matter problem, the problem of understanding the relation between mind and matter, has brought human understanding to an *impasse*. The question is how something describable in physical, spatiotemporal terms, such as neuronal activity, can relate to something that cannot be described spatiotemporally, such as melancholy or curiosity. We know that mind and matter can be correlated, but *we do not know the nature of that correlation*. Psycho-neural identity theory asserts that a mental state simply *is* its correlated brain state, but a problem therewith is *multiple realization*: a mental state such as hunger can be correlated to a human brain state but also presumably to, say, an octopus brain state,[13] thus indicating that the mental state cannot be identical to a human brain state. A more popular proposed solution today is *emergentism*: that mental states *emerge* from physical states. The problem here is that there are no known 'bridge laws' that could describe how such emergence takes place (how physical movement could transition into that which is not physically describable), not to mention the problem of *mental causation*, as we shall see below. There are other more extreme proposed solutions to the mind-matter problem, such as *physicalist eliminativism* which denies the existence of mind, and its contrary *subjective idealism* which denies the existence of matter. Though the first appears oxymoronic, and the latter darkly solipsistic, whatever the solution to the problem is, we know it will be radical. From this background map of mind-matter cul-de-sacs, panpsychism begins to be seen as a potentially clear exit road which may lead to a more comprehensive and parsimonious view of reality. But let us navigate through three[14] arguments for panpsychism to decipher it as a route to truth.

These following arguments – briefly: that the mental cannot emerge from 'matter', that 'matter' is but an abstraction, and that the brain is not a necessary condition for mentality – will be elucidated by combining and augmenting the thoughts of various thinkers. Thereafter certain reasons for the rejection of panpsychism will be considered – reasons histrionic, philosophic, cultural, and historic. Ultimately my intention is not merely to inform the reader as to what panpsychism is and why it is held, but to instill in the reader the cognizance that this mind-matter theory is not only an option that is serious, but one that is most plausible.

1. The Genetic Argument

If one does *not* believe in panpsychism,[15] then one believes that sentience at one point in time emerged from, had its genesis in, insentient matter (lest it emerge from something non-physical).[16] By implication, if one *does* believe in panpsychism (P), one believes that sentience always existed with matter – and thus never emerged at a point in time, but was always intrinsic thereto. Thus if we reject such emergentism (E),[17] we thereby advocate panpsychism: ~E = P.

Why should we reject the popular theory of emergentism? Eminent philosopher of mind, Jaegwon Kim has claimed that, '[it] is no undue exaggeration to say that we have been under the reign of emergentism since the early 1970s'.[18] However, despite being known as one of the greatest exponents of emergentism, Kim is wary of its truth:

> The idea of emergence is an attractive, and initially appealing, one in many ways, and it is not difficult to understand its popularity. But it is not easy to make the idea precise and give it substantive content.[19]

It is easy to say that mind emerges from certain, say, neurological activities in the brain. But substantiating what this word 'emerges' actually means and implies in such statements is far from easy. That a whirlpool emerges from water, or that water emerges from H_2O molecules are examples of emergence that can be observed and explained using *structural*, i.e. primarily spatiotemporal, language. But that the patterned movement of particles in a brain makes emerge mental states that *cannot* be observed or described in structural, spatiotemporal terms, is a claim that is *not scientific*: it is not directly observable, it is not quantifiable, and there is no known transordinal nomology: no bridge laws that would explain the matter-mind emergence (laws that would have to cover more than the human species). One cannot 'zoom into' an emotion to observe that from which it has emerged – as one can zoom into a whirlpool or into water – thus applying the emergence observed in Nature to explain the mind is a disanalogy, a category mistake.[20] We cannot simply infer that as chemistry emerges from physics, and as biology emerges from chemistry, so sentience emerges from biology. No: *there are no known laws of nature that can render explicable the emergence of emotion from motion, of sentience from insentience.*

Furthermore, emergentism, as a physicalist doctrine, cannot accommodate *mental causation* (that mental events such as desire can have an effect upon the world) – *as mentality is not an accepted force of Nature* – yet most emergentists do not want to fall into *epiphenomenalism* (that mental states are powerless aftereffects of physical activity, the mere steam of a locomotive engine[21]). Not being able to accept nor reject mental causation is to have your cake and eat it, which is essentially a *reductio ad absurdum*, a reduction to absurdity, thus a fatal wound inflicted upon emergentism. Even Isaac Newton allowed for the possibility of mental causation, and with it the suggestion of panpsychism:

> We find in ourselves a power of moving our bodies by our thoughts … and see the same power in other living creatures but how this is done and by what laws we do not know. … It appears that there are other laws of motion … [and this is] enough to justify and encourage our search after them. We cannot say that all of nature is not alive.[22]

If mental causation did not exist, i.e. if epiphenomenalism were the case, then the activity of reasoning – of working things out – would be useless; our desires, beliefs, and ambitions would be without efficacy in the world. Karl Popper, whose philosophy of science has had a large effect upon science through his notion of falsificationism, argued that epiphenomenalism is an *anti-evolutionary theory*.[23] If the mind had no power it would not have evolved nor survived, not only in us humans but presumably in other organisms as well. Sentience serves us well, but this implies that the dead physicalist ontology upon which emergentism is founded is flawed.

Moreover, emergentism is anti-evolutionary not only because it cannot account for mental causation but also because it implies an inexplicable jump in evolution. As William James stated,

> Consciousness, however small, is an illegitimate birth in any philosophy that starts without it, and yet professes to explain all facts by continuous evolution.

> If evolution is to work smoothly, consciousness in some shape must have been present at the very origin of things.[24]

There would be a monumental jump in the universe even with the simplest emergence of sentience: there would be a point in time, presumably concurrent with an organism, where there suddenly pierced into reality some kind of entity – with its own perspective – that was no longer merely structurally describable. This would have been an emergence of kind rather than an emergence of degree. For such a claim, *the burden of proof* lies upon the person who believes it rather than upon the panpsychist who denies its occurrence. The panpsychological position that there was no 'big pang of consciousness', as one may call it, is the default position of the person who will not endorse such an extreme position for which the evidence of change is lacking.

The founder of population genetics, evolutionist Sewall Wright, puts the case stronger still, claiming that:

> [The evolution of a] new organ ... involves nothing more mysterious than differential growth ... . Emergence of [this kind] ... poses no serious philosophical difficulty. Emergence of mind from no mind at all is *sheer magic*. ... [M]ind must already have been there when life arose and indeed must be a universal aspect of existence...[25]

Wright points out that this alleged emergence would present the occurrence of *magic* not only during the course of evolution, but even during each pregnancy:

> The emergence of mind in the course of individual development from the fertilized egg presents a similar problem and one that is an everyday occurrence instead of a single event in the remote past. It would appear that the mind of a human being must develop from something of the nature of mind in the fertilized egg and, back of this, in the separate germ cells and in the nucleic acid molecules.[26]

Sewall Wright was not the only renowned biologist who realized the genetic rationale for panpsychism: the founder of epigenetics, follower of Whitehead, C. H. Waddington also expressed the sentiment:

> The idea that something of the same general kind as self-awareness may exist in inanimate systems is one which ... is forced upon us by the demands of logic and the application of the evolutionary theory...[27]

To summarize: emergentism cannot explain 'upward causation' (matter-mind emergence) nor 'downward causation' (as mental causation). If we consequently reject emergentism, if we reject the notion that mind emerged and emerges from matter, *then we* ipso facto *accept that mind always existed with matter: panpsychism* – or, that it emerged from something other than matter such as a god. But let us leave the gods to themselves, and realize once more why panpsychism is not a religious stance based on faith, but a stance rooted in reason.

2. The Abstraction Argument

This argument advances the claim that our common notion of matter, or physicality, is merely an abstraction – that is, an incomplete understanding – that as such only exhibits certain external, *structural* (primarily spatial) properties to the exclusion of concrete intrinsic[28] properties, which are properties of sentience. *Understanding matter structurally is akin to understanding a scallop as being merely its shell – panpsychism sees the inner life.*

Schopenhauer claimed that the mind-matter problem was first discovered by Descartes.[29] Descartes' concept of matter was austere in that it was sufficiently characterized by a single property: *extension* (spatiality).[30] This, Thomas Kuhn claims,[31] triggered the mechanistic understanding of nature (physicalism as *mechanism*). As our knowledge advanced over time, further properties were attributed to matter such as nuclear force, mass, decay, spin, subatomic differentials,[32] and so on.

So we realize that former conceptions of matter were abstract as they excluded properties which we now consider essential to what matter *is*. Yet there is no reason to believe that we have reached a sufficiency in our understanding of matter, as 'pessimistic induction'[33] reveals.

Moreover, despite such advances in physics, we still inherit the Cartesian dualist dichotomy of the fundamental separateness of matter and mind. A. N. Whitehead laments this predicament by stating:

> The disastrous separation of body and mind which has been fixed on European thought by Descartes is responsible for this blindness of science.[34]

The mechanical physicalism of science seeks ultimately to reduce mind to matter; idealism seeks to reduce matter to mind, but panpsychism seeks to fuse Descartes' division by placing mind *in* matter. This means attributing to matter intrinsic, non-structural properties. A popular modern strand of panpsychism trades by the name 'Russellian Monism',[35] due to Bertrand Russell's thoughts on such attribution:

> [P]hysical events are known only as regards their space-time structure. The qualities that compose such events are unknown – so completely unknown that we cannot say either that they are, or that they are not, different from the qualities that we know as belonging to mental events.[36]

That is to say that we perceive certain outer structural, or relational, features of the matter surrounding us – e.g. an object's size, shape, location, velocity, etc. – and can speculate whether, (a) matter has further intrinsic properties, known as 'quiddities',[37] to which we are not privy,[38] and (b) whether such possible intrinsic properties are sentient in nature. We do have reason to suppose that there are such intrinsic properties which are sentient. In the words of David Chalmers:

> There is only one class of intrinsic, nonrelational property with which we have any direct familiarity, and that is the class of phenomenal properties.[39]

T. L. S. Sprigge goes a step further in proclaiming that:

> [If] the physical world has an inner being (as it must have, if it is not merely phenomenal, that is, a convenient fiction), that inner being must be psychical [sentient] if it is to be anything intelligible at all...[40]

Even Friedrich Nietzsche pushes this point in a causal manner:

> The *mechanistic world* is thus imagined as the senses of vision and touch alone could envisage such a world (as in 'motion'), so as to be predictable ... [but] the will to power, which is not a being, not a becoming, but a *pathos*, is the most elementary fact ... . Mechanics ... does not so much touch the question of the nature of causal force.[41]

In sum, the mechanical, physicalist ideology only presents matter's structure but not its content.

We see that the notion of matter has evolved through history, from certain Ancient Greek elements through to modern age matter-energy identities and quantum-physic oddities. It would not be prudent, viewing that history, to believe that we have today finally reached a complete, concrete knowledge of *what matter is*. It would be more imprudent still to believe that we can explain sentience through this current (deficient) understanding of matter, which is why the hard problem of consciousness is hard. In order to soften it, we can *expand our notion of matter* to include the internal aspect of the matter that we at least can be certain exists for ourselves: sentience. A full physical description of your body and behaviour will *not* be a full description of yourself: it will omit your sentience. Rather than be anthropocentric and reserve such sentience to ourselves, and in order to avoid the impasse of claiming the emergence of mind from dead, insentient matter, one achieves greater parsimony by attributing basic forms of sentience to all matter. In this way, mind does not magically emerge from matter but is always part of matter, and the dichotomy between them is thereby seen to be false. All of reality is alive, it is our conceptualization that creates the illusion that most of nature is dead, that the shell alone is the organism. This is a mistake due to committing what Whitehead calls 'the fallacy of misplaced concreteness'. Even a corpse will contain a multiplicity of sentiences, though no longer unified by the higher, deceased one. Echoing the sentiment of Schopenhauer's line that begins this article, Whitehead claimed that:

> It is the accepted doctrine in physical science that a living body is to be interpreted according to what is known of other sections of the physical universe. This is a sound axiom, but it is double-edged. For it carries with it the converse deduction that other sections of the universe are to be interpreted in accordance with what we know of the human body.[42]

This is essentially to say that our current form of science is not equipped to respond to the mind-matter problem. This is why we must seek more sufficient answers in metaphysics, and beyond proof we must employ *abductive reasoning* (inference to the best explanation) rather than inductive empirical verification. As one cannot directly observe the sentience of another, the scientific method is here not sufficient as it is based on the experience of structure, not the experience of other experience. Just as science cannot prove matters in mathematics or logic, so it cannot prove matters in metaphysics – and panpsychism is a metaphysical theory. Understand: *the demand for empirical proof for mind-matter theories can only deliver solipsism*, as one can here only strictly prove that one's own consciousness exists.[43] Fortunately, knowledge transcends that gained by empirical proof.

3. The Inferential Argument

In outline, this argument advocates the position that one cannot consistently infer the existence of sentience in humans and other animals without inferring it to exist within *all* natural entities: panpsychism.

We infer that other humans have sentience. Perhaps, as some have argued,[44] we can directly experience others' sentience. But even if this is so, we can only infer that humans with whom we have not been in contact are sentient.[45] Most of us infer sentience in certain non-human animals. Descartes is possibly an exception to this as he considered animals to be automata (though he was not consistent as he also attributed feelings to magpies).[46] However, as we cannot acquire the report of consciousness from animals, we cannot establish direct neural correlates of consciousness (as this requires *both* mind and matter correlates). Thus our assumption of their sentience is not based on neurology so much as behaviour. Consider, especially, the octopus: its brain, two-thirds of which lie in its arms, is very dissimilar to our brain, yet the intelligent behaviour of the sea creature renders a denial of sentience to it implausible. Thus we do attribute sentience to it though *we do not have a strict criterion* by which we do so. So we can *but infer sentience rather than verify it*, and people will differ in their guessed inferences: some might stop sentience at the lobster limit, others might stop at the beetle border, but why stop at all? If one demands a stop, the determining criterion must be established.

If one proposes the criterion that a being can *sense* and *adapt to its environment*, then one has almost become panpsychist by allowing for the sentience of plants. For instance, biologist Daniel Chamovitz writes that:

> [We] now know that *Arabidopsis [thaliana]* has at least eleven different photoreceptors: some tell a plant when to germinate, some tell it when to bend to the light, some tell it when to flower, and some let it know when it's night time. Some let the plant know that there's a lot of light hitting it, some let it know that the light is dim, and some help it to keep time.[47]

Thus eyes are not required to perceive light, just as muscles are not required to move. Therefore if one wants a criterion that rules out plants as sentient, it cannot be based on the ability to sense or adapt. So a more commonly-held, stricter criterion for sentience is the possession of a complex nervous system, or a *brain*. One may believe this to be the case because one can gauge *correlations* between human brain events and mental events, via brain scans, brain damage, drug use, etc. Hence this mistaken argument:

1. If brain then sentience.
   [Based on human neural correlates of consciousness.]
2. No brain. [E.g. in a plant.]
3. Therefore, no sentience. [I.e. in the plant.]

But this argument is an obvious example of *the fallacy of denying the antecedent* (P → Q, ~P, ∴~Q).[48] It is equivalent to arguing that if you drink hemlock you will die, you did not drink hemlock, therefore you will not die (an easy way to acquire immortality!). Just as there could be other ways to die other than by hemlock, so there could be other ways to have sentience other than by having a brain.

The philosopher Friedrich Paulsen, following the lead of renowned panpsychist and founder of psychophysics, Gustav Theodor Fechner, puts the point this way:

> With what functions, with what marks that are lacking in plants, is inner life [sentience] connected?—Reference is made to the absence of a nervous system and brain. … [But] the syllogism is worthless. It is formulated on the plan: Horses dogs, and cats have legs, without which they cannot move; therefore creatures without legs cannot move. Snakes and worms contradict the syllogism.[49]

There may be other systematic substrata of matter that correlate to sentience other than those of the animal brain. If one believes in the possibility of machine, or robot sentience, one cannot disagree. Plants do not have neurons but they have other parts by which they transmit information, as do single-celled organisms, viruses, molecules and more. The point is made by the distinguished mycologist Paul Stamets about fungi, a kingdom more related to animals than to plants:

> I see mycelium [mushrooms' root network] as ... an exposed sentient membrane, aware and responsive to changes in its environment. As hikers, deer, or insects walk across these sensitive filamentous nets, they leave impressions, and mycelia sense and respond to these movements.[50]

That human sentience is correlated with neural activity (the neural correlates of consciousness) is not sufficient to establish a *necessary* condition for sentience, it only establishes a *contingent* condition. A human brain may be necessary for *human* consciousness,[51] but it cannot be deemed necessary for consciousness, let alone sentience. While an orchestra is necessary for a symphony, it is not necessary for music generally, let alone sound.

Thus we have no logical reason to limit the inference of sentience to creatures with brains. And if we limit the inference to behaviour or sensation, we would then have to include plants, fungi, viruses, and other microbes as well. This is thus nearing panpsychism already. Karl Popper relates the remarks of biologist H. S. Jennings, claiming that 'in observing the behaviour of the amoeba, [Jennings] could hardly help attributing to it consciousness'.[52] Now someone might retort that though such behaviour looks as if it were conscious, it can nonetheless be described solely by physical mechanism. But this is a weak retort because one could also describe a human solely by physical mechanism (the movement of nerve impulses, neurotransmitters, muscle contraction, etc.), yet this would not thereby refute the existence of the human's sentience.

It may be further retorted that though we may justifiably attribute sentience to organisms, we do not have the justification to transgress this limit to include sentience within the *inorganic*. Though an amoeba would have a touch of sentience, a molecule would not. This response is conditioned by a belief that there is a natural dichotomy between the organic and the inorganic. This assumption is rejected by thinkers such as Leibniz[53] and Whitehead, and is the reason for the latter naming his metaphysics 'the philosophy of organism'. This philosophy is encapsulated within his line that, 'Biology is the study of the larger organisms; whereas physics is the study of the smaller organisms.'[54]

This is to say that there is no natural delineation between what we call the living and the non-living: if we attribute sentience to a fungus, to a cell, to a virus, to an 'organic molecule', then the continuation to other types of molecule with their quasi-autopoietic, systematic maintained characteristics and behaviour faces no natural barrier[55] (though not all aggregates are such 'organisms': clouds and cliffs are not sentient as such, but are collections of comprising sentiences/organisms). Consequently, as we have no criterion by which we can stop the inference attributing sentience to creatures without brains, nor to the so-called 'inorganic' – and as we *do have* a reason to extend it down (to avoid the magic of emergentism and epiphenomenalism [the Genetic Argument], and to bestow an immanence to structural matter [the Abstraction Argument]) – the inference of sentience is extended all the way down through Nature: panpsychism.

Why Panpsychism is Spurned

Above are but three intertwined arguments for maintaining that mind, in at least its simpler forms, is found beyond the brain, in simpler entities. Once one becomes accustomed to the idea, its logic and parsimony, the incredulous stares one receives for accepting panpsychism are met with the same repose as that from the stares an evolutionist might receive from a medieval Christian congregation. Why is panpsychism spurned today if it holds such rationale? I shall outline a few possibilities here.

Firstly there are common misunderstandings about what panpsychism is, and therefore it is often the victim of the straw man fallacy. Panpsychism does not maintain that chairs, tables, gates or stables, are sentient as such, as unified entities. There are no self-conscious sofas, contemplating their contemptuous, servile existence. Almost five hundred years ago, Giordano Bruno already made the point that one must distinguish between *natural unified entities* as those having mind, and aggregates of such units.[56] The distinction is common in the literature: Leibniz called such units *monads*, Whitehead called them *organisms*, Arthur Koestler called them *holons*.[57]

Another common misunderstanding is a belief in the success of alternate mind-matter theories. There is no agreed upon mind-matter theory and thus no default position to which to have recourse. Even amongst the more physicalist-centred mind-matter theories there exists a plethora of conflicting views such as eliminativism, behaviourism, functionalism, identity theory, biological naturalism, epiphenomenalism, anomalous monism, and emergentism. None of these are without serious problems, and so panpsychism does not challenge any *established* alternate view.

Related to this misunderstanding is the belief, as mentioned, that a mind-matter theory needs to provide empirical 'proof' to be acceptable. This is partly a legacy of the now discredited epistemology of Verificationism.[58] If this demand for proof were accepted, then no mind-matter theory bar solipsism would be acceptable.[59] And if one considers solipsism unacceptable, then the demand for empirical proof is not required for a mind-matter theory such as panpsychism. In matters of the mind we move from science to metaphysics, from verification to inference to the best explanation.

A more rational reason for spurning panpsychism is recognition of its inherent problematic issues, the most significant of which is known as 'the combination problem':[60] how it is possible for a multiplicity of sentiences to combine to form a unified sentience. This is an old problem stated by Ralph Cudworth in 1678,[61] and even Immanuel Kant in 1766.[62] There are numerous proposed solutions to this problem, foremost perhaps is its effacement through Whitehead's metaphysical system.[63] We cannot enter the details of this issue here,[64] but we can annul the problem as one specifically detrimental to panpsychism by highlighting the point that the combination problem is also a problem for physicalism. Thus *if we reject panpsychism because of the combination problem we must thereby reject physicalism as well*. As David Chalmers writes:

> Of course physicalism is faced with its own version of the combination problem: How do microphysical entities and properties come together to yield subjects, qualities, and so on? This challenge is presumably at least as hard as the challenge to panpsychism…[65]

Another more basic criticism of panpsychism is that it is blatant *anthropomorphism*: attributing human characteristics (i.e. mentality) to non-human entities. There are two simple responses to this. Firstly, to attribute to Nature the characteristic of being akin to that of man-made machines (mechanism) is also anthropomorphic – so the accusation cuts both ways. Secondly, to charge panpsychism with anthropomorphism is itself to commit *anthropocentrism*: to believe that we are unique, special in our sentience. To have such prejudgement is of course *to beg the question* against panpsychism.

If we move back to view more historic reasons for the spurning of panpsychism, Descartes' legacy comes into view. As quoted earlier, Whitehead blames Descartes' mind-matter dualism for the blindness of today's science. This may at first seem an odd accusation as current science mostly rejects such a dualism that posits the existence of a soul. However, Whitehead's point is that though the common scientific creed rejected Descartes' notion of soul or mind, *it accepted Descartes' notion that Nature itself was devoid of mind*, being mere dead, mathematically-describable, mechanism. This dead, structural view of nature has been instrumental in the success of the technological progress of the industrial nations, but by removing mind from matter this view has reached the impasse signaled by the 'hard problem of consciousness': one cannot regain mind from the mechanical matter from which it was expelled, one cannot regain the concrete from the abstraction. Trying to extract mind from this dead, abstract view of matter is as feasible as trying to extract apple juice from an oil painting of an orchard. Despite such difficulties, this view of 'normal' science became prevalent, with the consequence that panpsychism (where mind is part of matter rather than a product thereof) became heresy. The life of mentality had to submit to the laws of motion. Thomas S. Kuhn puts the predicament thus:

> Normal science … is an attempt to force nature into the preformed and relatively inflexible box that the paradigm supplies … . [After Descartes], laws had to specify corpuscular motion and interaction, and explanation had to reduce any given natural phenomenon to corpuscular action under these laws.[66]

Strictly speaking, panpsychism is contrary to *scientism* rather than to *science* (if we take science to be a method rather than a dogma). Regardless, panpsychism, as well as transgressing the general scientific paradigm, transgresses the Christian one. Living under the shadow of both science and Christianity should make us wise to the legacy and interaction between the two, which is not always as antagonistic as is often believed. Descartes' explicit aim in his *Meditations on First Philosophy* – wherein he divided Nature into human souls and the mechanistic environment in which they find themselves – was to carry out the call of Pope Leo X to prove that the soul (which Descartes equated to mind) was distinct to the material body, in order to support the doctrine of life after death. Panpsychism *per se* does not need to make this afterlife claim: the death of the body implies the dissolution of the unifying sentience (the dominant monad, the holon) into its still unified smaller components, but the self as such dies. In panpsychism, mankind has no special status distinct from the other organisms, and as such is generally opposed to Christianity[67] and other Abrahamic religions. Moreover, panpsychism is more akin to the animistic, pagan religions that worshipped Nature. Thus in Christendom, panpsychism has been contrary to both the religious and mechanistic ethos, resulting in it being shunned, disdained, and perhaps even purposefully suppressed:

the Roman Inquisition burned the panpsychist Giordano Bruno on the stake in 1600.

The Whiteheadian philosopher Charles Hartshorne suggests that another more banal reason for the 'disinclination of many to accept psychicalism [panpsychism] probably arises partly from the immense demands which the doctrine make upon one's imagination'.[68] It is no easy feat to imagine the mind of a mantis, maple, or molecule, or to fathom what it is like to be a bat or a boson. But Hartshorne calls this error of dismissal due to imaginative failure *the prosaic fallacy*: 'supposing the world to be as tame as our sluggish convention-ridden imaginations imply'.[69] If the prosaic fallacy is a reason for the rejection of panpsychism then at least *there is an antidote, and quite literally a chemical antidote*. William James, who at first criticized panpsychism, primarily by invoking the combination problem,[70] but who eventually came to accept and promote the theory,[71] gave guidance on how to transcend prosaic consciousness through psychoactive drugs.[72]

End Remarks

The rejection of panpsychism can be overcome by logical analysis, historical and cultural reflection, and perhaps even by chemical ingestion. Logical analysis reveals the fatal flaws of physicalist mind-matter theories against which I have juxtaposed panpsychism as an alternate rational, parsimonious approach. The approaches of dualism and idealism can be seen as alternates to panpsychism too, but certain varieties are complementary. For instance, Karl Popper claimed that 'Schopenhauer is a Kantian who has turned panpsychist',[73] a phrase indicating the compatibility of his transcendental idealism and panpsychism. Schopenhauer's work certainly shows the merits of genius, yet I believe that the greatest riches in the search for a satisfactory mind-matter theory will be unearthed with inspiration from the work of Alfred North Whitehead, 'the most distinguished champion of panpsychism in the twentieth century'.[74]

Notes

1. Schopenhauer, 1844/1966, ch. XVIII, p. 196.
2. A term introduced in 1591 by Francesco Patrizi in *Nova de universis philosophia* (New Philosophy of the Universe).
3. Or 'mind' (singular) if minds (plural) are constituents of an overmind in the sense of Mainonides' or Spinoza's 'infinite intellect'. See Sjöstedt-Hughes, 2022.
4. In other words, non-reductively.
5. By actuality I mean physicality. This thus excludes other purported non-physical modes of existence, such as the realm of universals posited by thinkers such as Frege, Russell, Santayana, Whitehead, et al.
6. *Animism* is a word made popular by anthropologist Edward B. Tylor (1871). Tylor acknowledges that the *word* 'animism' had already been in use – but existed with different meanings (Tylor, p. 384, fn. 1).
7. Though panpsychism takes the reality of matter to be insufficiently understood, as we shall see.
8. I write 'generally' because there are idealist and dualist varieties of panpsychism.
9. With the note that physicalism allows sentience to a small fragment of matter, namely that involved in complex interaction such as brains. Note also that, unlike me, panpsychist Galen Strawson classifies panpsychism as physicalism (2006).
10. Plato, 1965, p. 103 (*Timaeus*, §41:77).
11. For a comprehensive overview of panpsychological thinkers, see Skrbina, 2007.
12. Chalmers, 1996.
13. See Putnam, 1975, pp. 436–7.
14. Though there are more than three arguments for panpsychism.
15. Or at least in 'psychism': the view that some matter has always had mind but not all.
16. *Neutral monism*, or *Panprotopsychism*, in general claims that mind and matter both emerged from a common 'neutral' source. *Idealism* can claim that as the mind produces time, there was no time before the mind in which it could have emerged. Thirdly, *theistic dualism* claims that mind emerged not from matter but from God. We shall leave these options aside.
17. There are really two forms of emergentism spoken of here: the general historic and the specific, but the the distinction makes no difference to our argument. Psycho-neural identity theory would be part of the former (as brains emerged in time) but not the latter (as the specific form of emergentism does not see the mind and brain as [at least epistemically] identical).
18. Kim, 2010, p. 10.
19. Kim, 2006, p. 559.
20. D. R. Griffin calls the disanalogy the 'Emergence Category Mistake' (1998, p. 65).

21 This was the analogy of Thomas Huxley who advocated epiphenomenalism.
22 *Opticks*, Q22. Quoted in Skrbina, p. 93.
23 Popper, 1977; 1978.
24 James, 1890, Ch. VI, p. 149. In this chapter, James proceeds to refute the panpsychist theory he at first posits ('the mind-stuff theory'). However, later (1909/2008) he accepts panpsychism.
25 Pt. 3, ch. 2, in: Cobb, J. B. and Griffin, D. R., eds. (1977). My emphasis.
26 Ibid.
27 Waddington, 1961, p. 122.
28 'Intrinsic' meant in a metaphorical rather than in a literal, spatial, sense.
29 1844, ch. XVIII, p. 192.
30 See Nagel, 1961/1974, p. 171.
31 1962/1970, ch. IX, p. 104.
32 See Feigl, 1958 and Nagel, 1961/1974, p. 370, *et passim*.
33 See Laudan, 1981.
34 Whitehead, 1938/1968, p. 154.
35 See Alter and Nagasawa, 2012.
36 Russell, 1948/2009, p. 204.
37 See Chalmers, 2016, p. 26.
38 To employ the previous metaphor: the scallop's internal anatomy.
39 Chalmers, 2016, p. 153.
40 Sprigge, 1994, p. 86.
41 Nietzsche, 2017, p. 362 (§635). See also §36 of Nietzsche, 1886/2008. (It was Nietzsche who led me to panpsychism.)
42 Whitehead, 1929/1985, p. 110 (Ch. IV, §5).
43 The possibility that one can directly experience others' consciousness is a possibility rejected by the positivists who demand 'proof', so its possibility is here ignored.
44 For example, Henri Bergson and A. N. Whitehead.
45 With the possible exclusion of those in dreamless sleep, and others suffering unconsciousness (in a coma, etc.).
46 See Cottingham, 1978 for a discussion on Descartes' inconsistency here.
47 Chamovitz, 2012, pp. 25–26.
48 Note that if one reverses the conditional claim to 'if one has sentience, then one has a brain' ($Q \to P$), one thereby commits the fallacy *petitio principii* (begging the question) against panpsychism.
49 Paulsen, 1895, pp. 96–97.
50 Stammets, 2005, p. 4.

51 Even this is questionable when one considers examples such as the Lorber case (see Lewin, 1980), where it was discovered that a 'normal', intelligent mathematics' student had virtually no brain.

52 Popper, 1978, p. 352. Note that Popper himself was critical of panpsychism (1977).

53 Expressed in lines such as 'Even if not all bodies are organic, nevertheless organic bodies lie hidden in everything ... organisms are everywhere, and nowhere is there chaos unworthy of wisdom...' ('Against Barbaric Physics', in Leibniz, 1989, p. 319).

54 Whitehead, 1925/1967, p. 103 (Ch. VI).

55 Whitehead argues that even subatomic entities prehend their environment and adapt accordingly (1929/1978).

56 In *Cause, Principle, and Unity* (1584), §44: 'the table is not animated as a table, nor are clothes as clothes ... but that, as natural things and composites, they have within matter and form [i.e. soul]. All things, no matter how small and miniscule, have in them part of that spiritual substance ... For in all things there is spirit, and there is not the least corpuscle that does not contain within itself some portion that may animate it'.

57 See Koestler, 1978.

58 A view common in the early twentieth century that claimed that a proposition was only meaningful if it was either true by definition or empirically verifiable in principle.

59 I exclude the absurd theories that deny mind altogether, such as behaviourism.

60 Coined by William Seager, 1995.

61 Cudworth, 1678/1845: *The True Intellectual System of the Universe*.

62 Kant, 1766, p. 14 (Ch. 1, 2:328, fn.)

63 As concisely exposited by D. R. Griffin, 1998, pp. 177–181.

64 See the chapters on Whitehead's philosophy of organism, in this volume; and Sjöstedt-Hughes, 2016.

65 Chalmers, 2016, p. 39.

66 Kuhn, 1962, pp. 21, 41.

67 Though their harmony has been attempted – e.g. via Fechner.

68 Hartshorne, 1977: Ch.3:'Physics and Psychics: The Place of Mind in Nature', in Cobb & Griffin 1977.

69 Ibid.

70 James, 1890.

71 James, 1909/1920.

72 See *The Varieties of Religious Experience* (1902), lectures XVI and XVII; and the expansive endnote about nitrous oxide in 'On Some Hegelisms' (1882).

73 Popper, 1977, p. 68.

74 Edwards, 1967, p. 31 (in the entry on Panpsychism).

II

Conspectus of A. N. Whitehead's Metaphysics

Whitehead's metaphysics is a system of **panpsycho-panentheism**.
- I.e. a panpsychism: that all entities have sentience (or, 'proto-sentience'), combined with a panentheism: that God is Nature and more.

Whitehead calls his system the **Philosophy of Organism** or **Organic Realism**; it is also known as **Process Philosophy**.
- Every entity is an organism. There is no inorganic reality at the fundamental level.
- It is known as Process Philosophy because in actuality there are no static substances, but only events, occasions, processes.

The smallest processes are called **actual occasions**, or **actual entities**.
- These are drops of experience that constitute Nature.
- Actual entities are perspectives on the world, somewhat analogous to Leibniz's monads. They are transitory: they become and they perish.

The process of an actual entity is called a **concrescence** that involves an **initial subjective aim** to create that actual entity, a **prehension** of other actual entities and eternal objects, a **subjective aim** that conduces a **decision**, and a **satisfaction** that completes the process. These completed actual entities pass into **objective immortality**: data for present actual entities.

An initial subjective aim is bequeathed by the panentheistic God (see below) that sets off an experiential perspective.

An actual entity **prehends** other actual entities, but not in the traditional relation of representation-to-object but rather in the relation part-to-whole.
- I. e. the prehension of an actual entity is the actual inclusion of that other actual entity within itself.
- It is (except for negative prehensions, below) a *feeling*.
- This inclusive fusion is called **vectoring,** it is referred to by the **Principle of Relativity**. There is no absolute subject-object dichotomy.
- Prehensions of actual entities include those of the immediate *past*.

The universals that an actual entity employs for their prehensions are called **eternal objects**. These are metaphysical 'pure potentials' and subsist within a realm of 'God' (see below).

Prehensions can be positive or negative, physical or conceptual:
- **Positive prehensions** are of what is included in the actual entity.
- **Negative prehensions** reject entities and concepts for inclusion.
- **Physical prehensions** are of other actual entities.
- **Conceptual prehensions** are of eternal objects alone.
- There are also **impure** and **hybrid prehensions** which are combinations of the above.

An actual entity is determined by past prehensions, but it is also to varying extents self-determined through its subjective aim that strives for experiential *aesthetic intensity*.

There is thus *efficient causality* in the inheritance of the prehensions of actual entities, and *final causality* (teleology) in the subjective aim of actual entities.

Actual entities in aggregate are called **nexūs**, and if the nexūs share a common characteristic they are called **societies**.
- An electron is an example of a society, as is an atom, molecule, and crystal.

What are traditionally named 'organisms' are **complex societies**.

These high-grade societies **transmute** a plurality of incoming prehensions into an abstracted unity for ease of comprehension. Common human sense perception is an example thereof.

There are two main species of human perception: **perception in the mode of causal efficacy** (PMCE) and **perception in the mode of presentational immediacy** (PMPI):

- PMPI is commonly identified with all perception, being that from the 'five senses'.
- PMCE is the less distinct yet more ubiquitous internal experience of the actions and experiences of the past and concurrent surroundings flowing into the present.

God is vital for the operations of Whitehead's system. God has two natures: the primordial and the consequent:
- **The primordial nature of God** (PNG) is the realm of eternal objects.
    - The eternal objects are *ingressed* into all our experiences thereby determining the qualitative type of the experience.
- **The consequent nature of God** (CNG) is the pantheistic unity of all experiences drawn into one higher consciousness.
- PNG is unconscious; CNG is conscious.

God bestows the initial subjective aim for an actual entity as a *lure* for its *concresence* and the experiential intensity it evokes.
- It is God's purpose to enjoy the experiential intensities God provokes.

God is not omnipotent as actual entities and their societies have their own teleology.

God is not omniscient because the future does not yet exist because novelty emerges from actualities via their subjective aim and the infinity of eternal objects.

God is not omnibenevolent because morality is subordinate to aesthetic appreciation which is God's desire.

(Thus 'God' is perhaps a misnomer.)

Above Actual Entities and God, the third main tenet of Whitehead's cosmology is **Creativity**.

- o God conditions creativity but it is beyond His control.

All but the PNG is subject to flux, to process, to novelty, to creativity.

- o Matter evolves as well as 'organisms', the laws of nature change accordingly, even the three dimensions of our extensive epoch will pass into history and in its place a cosmos of unimaginable difference will arise.

― ― ―

III

The Concrescence of Dissent
Whitehead as Religious, Scientific, Philosophic Heretic

Philosopher Alfred North Whitehead's career can be glimpsed through trinities: Cambridge,[1] London, Harvard; mathematician, philosopher of science, metaphysician; and, dispersed through these, the trinity that is Anglican, agnostic, heretic. Further still, his heresy covers the tripartite of religion, science, and philosophy. In order to fathom the transition Whitehead made from his family Anglicanism, to his agnosticism, through to his mature heretical systematic cosmology, we will first look at the environment in which he was raised and educated. We shall see how his rejection of the Church was in concurrence with the ideological flow of the times, and congruent with his adventurous yet critical questioning spirit. This antithetical rejection of religion lasted for only two decades. Due to personal tragedy and rational insight, Whitehead emerged from his agnostic chrysalis to new heights of metaphysics, a new philosophy yet in the old grand style – a philosophy that would make the Church look stagnantly infantile, science superfluously blind, and contemporary philosophy trivial and dry. This transition into metaphysics was, by this stage, not concurrent but counter to the cultural current. Whitehead did not oppose religion, science, and philosophy, he rather presented their greater potential. He was not an unbeliever in any of these three modes of thought, merely a heretic with regard to them, through his refutations of their stifling dogmas. Opposed to dogma, Whitehead chose free choice.

The word 'heresy' derives from the Greek word for 'choice', αἵρεσις, antedating its meaning of *choosing a school of thought*, that is, a religious or philosophical *sect*.[2] In English versions of the New Testament the word is variously translated as 'heresy' or 'sect' – always in a derogative manner as all Christians were to be considered as *one body*: the Church as the body of Christ (John 17:20–3; 1 Corinthians 12:12–14). The concept of heresy, however, predates Christianity as can be witnessed by reading Plato's late tome, *The Laws*, which prescribes imprisonment and death for heresy against state-ordained polytheism, 'forbidding religious activity without the blessing of the laws.'[3] Contrasting Plato and the Church, we see that the concept of heresy is *relative* to an *orthodoxy*: that is, relative to a set of opinions deemed by an authority as correct.[4] Milton espoused this relativism, decrying that:

> Men whose life, learning, faith and pure intent
> Would have been held in high esteem with Paul
> Must now be named and printed heretics…[5]

Beyond religion, we encounter orthodoxy in science and in philosophy, and in his tilting rather than rejecting of these cultural pillars, we shall see Whitehead as the arch-heretic, the hæresiarch of the twentieth century.

Part I: Life

Whitehead was born in 1861 in Kent: at Ramsgate in the Isle of Thanet – a stretch of land jutting out at the south-east of England. In its close proximity to the continent, this isle acted as the entry point for invading Romans, Teutons, and an assortment of other pagans and Christians, sinners and saints, through the ages. Whitehead was raised within a strongly Anglican family. His father and grandfather were both priests in the Church of England, as were two uncles, one of whom was a follower of the theologian and founder of Christian socialism, F. D. Maurice. Whitehead was the youngest of four siblings; his brother Henry became Bishop of Madras, an important diocese in India – first as a strict Tractarian, then as a more welcoming and open Ecumenical.[6] [7] In Whitehead's brief 'Autobiographical Notes' (1941), he speculates that his family came from the Quaker George Whitehead, who lived in Kent on the Isle of Sheppey in the mid to late seventeenth century.[8] Bertrand Russell, Whitehead's Cambridge student, collaborator, and friend, quipped exaggeratedly that Whitehead's 'family came from Kent and had been clergymen ever since about the time of the landing of St Augustine in that county.'[9]

Educating Bertrand Russell was also something of family tradition: Whitehead's clerical father had been summoned in 1877 to convince a sceptical five-year-old Bertrand Russell that the Earth was in fact spherical despite the evidence of the senses.[10] Within Rev. Whitehead's parish lay the summer residence of the Archbishop of Canterbury, Archibald Campbell Tait – a good friend of Whitehead's father and a figure whom the young Whitehead admired: 'Tait was a very great man. He should have been Prime Minister of Great Britain.'[11] Tait was a progressive force within the Church: a friend of science, a forgiver of Dissenters, and an opponent of the Oxford Movement which sought to ritualize the Anglican Church back to a form more traditional, more Roman Catholic or at least more pre-Reformation English. Tait introduced the 1874 Public Worship Regulation Act that curtailed this movement, thereby making a number of enemies. Whitehead was thus raised in a religious yet liberal environment. In 1875, he moved to a public boarding school in Sherborne, Dorset, which was run by a reverend and aimed to provide 'a liberal Education in accordance with the principles of the Church of England'.[12] When he entered Trinity College, Cambridge University in 1880 as a student of mathematics, he brought with him this particularly progressive, though nevertheless Anglican worldview.

In 1890, Whitehead married the highly-spirited aesthete Evelyn Wade and together they studied the history of Christianity for several years. He had been especially taken by the writings of John Henry Newman, who as a leader of the Oxford movement was an opponent of Tait. Newman's later conversion to Roman Catholicism was a shock to the high Anglican Church, and gave inspiration to Whitehead's near conversion to Roman Catholicism at that time. Though Whitehead rejected Cardinal Newman's religion, Newman's 'viewing of all religious philosophy under the category of life',[13] was, however, arguably influential in Whitehead's later organic, evolutionary philosophy of religion. At any rate, contrary to expectation, the result of these years of ecclesiastical study was *agnosticism*, a position reached a few years before the century's end.[14]

This agnosticism was not solely a product of religious exploration – it was also due to the collapse of science, or physics, as it was then understood. Whitehead's lessons at Cambridge were mathematical, with leanings toward physics. One of his teachers had been a pupil of James Clerk Maxwell, and of course at that time the 'Newtonian conceptions were still in full force.'[15] The later psychological reaction to the superseding of Newtonianism is of note, as it relates to Whitehead's apostasy.

> This experience has profoundly affected my thinking. To have supposed that you had certitude once, and certitude about the solidest-*looking* thing in the universe, and then to have had it

blow up on your hands into inconceivable infinities has affected everything else in the universe for me.[16]

The shift from Newtonian to Einsteinian physics inaugurated the twentieth century. Its psycho-cultural impact fostered a distrust of existing belief systems that mirrored the trajectory of Whitehead's thought.

Along with this crumbling certainty in science,[17] fell Whitehead's certainty in religion, an experience not uncommon at the time. The Church of England had been in decline from the early nineteenth century for various reasons. The theologian Rev. William Palmer, party to the Oxford Movement, claimed in 1845 that irreligion had been provoked by continental philosophers, most grievously by Voltaire, but was now 'insinuating itself under the disguise of charity, kindness, and liberality.'[18] This liberality meant a toleration of all faiths. In an Act of 1829, legal restrictions for Roman Catholics in England had been lifted. A few years thereafter, Parliament passed the 1834 Poor Law Amendment Act, which began to shift the responsibility of caring and educating the poor from Church to State. Indeed, numerous factors contributed to this decline in faith in addition to the aforementioned anti-religious philosophy. Such factors included the scientific rejection of certain Church beliefs such as that delivered by Darwin, the philological 'higher criticism' of the Bible, the displacement and alienation of parishioners due to the Industrial and Agricultural Revolutions, and the bitter distaste that much of the working class had for the corrupt decadence of English priests and the Church's unwritten yet evident allegiance if not alliance to the Tory political party.[19] Dissenters, such as the Methodists and Evangelicals, gained popularity because they represented the interests of the working class. All of these factors contributed to the fall in Anglican faith during the nineteenth and then twentieth centuries (with a later little two-pronged attack from Marx and Nietzsche).[20] In this respect, Whitehead's turn to agnosticism was not contrary to the cultural current of his time.

On a more personal level, Whitehead's loss of Christian faith also derived from his conversations with sceptical yet open-minded fellow students at Cambridge, especially within the secretive, high-intellectual *Cambridge Conversazione Society*, a group colloquially known as The Apostles.[21] This Society was founded in 1820 to introduce philosophic discussion to Cambridge, which at that time was centred narrowly around the natural theology of Rev. William Paley. The very nature and purpose of the society was to question religious dogma and established thought. Apostle and utilitarian philosopher, Henry Sidgwick, described the society thus:

> Absolute candour was the only duty that the tradition of the Society enforced. No consistency was demanded with opinions previously held – truth as we saw it then and there was what we had to embrace and maintain, and there were no propositions so well established that an Apostle had not the right to deny or question, if he did so sincerely and not from the love of mere paradox.[22]

Through this open method, the Apostles would fulfil one of the essential conditions of philosophy itself: to presuppose nothing.[23] Moreover, Whitehead considered the method and its execution as a refined quality of human life with political consequence: 'There is a strong [yet rare] moral intuition that speculative understanding for its own sake is one of the ultimate elements in a good life. The passionate claim for freedom of thought is based upon it.'[24] Whitehead was elected an Apostle in 1884. Two years later he nominated the Hegelian and atheist J. M. E. McTaggart, and in 1892 Whitehead ushered in Bertrand Russell.[25]

Each week an Apostle would pen a paper on a particular subject which the others would read in advance to discuss on the night. These discussions usually revolved around a closed question that would be voted upon at the session's cessation. Even though Whitehead was a practising Anglican till the very late 1880s, a number of the answers he gives to questions reveals a mind open to adventurous ideas, one not designated to be fettered by tradition. To provide a few examples:

> *'Shall we transcend our limitations?'* (1885)
> Whitehead: 'Yes', 'I want to see God.'
>
> *'Does the devil exist, or is he merely loathsome?'* (1885)
> Whitehead: 'Yes', to which he adds 'He is the Homogenous.'
>
> *'Have we a criterion for progress?'* (1886)
> Whitehead: 'No.'
>
> *'Should Churchmen go to Rome?'* (1886)
> Whitehead: ''Yes', 'or in the other direction.'
>
> *'Shall we read Hegel?'* (1887)
> Whitehead: 'No – but *I* shall.', '[U]rge others to do so and to read other metaphysicians as well.'[26]

The Apostles' wide-ranging discourse expanded Whitehead's mind beyond the mathematics he was researching, to matters cosmic, political, and personal. Even in mathematics, however, Whitehead was open-minded to the extent that he was amongst the first to teach non-Euclidean geometry at Cambridge, and devoted much of his first book *A Treatise on Universal Algebra* (1898) to the neglected theories of n-dimensional space developed by Hermann Günther Grassmann.[27] As a space of more than three dimensions was at first – wrongly – denigrated as incoherent and impractical, Whitehead's interest in this mathematical field betrays a progressive streak that would not be boxed into established axioms. At the beginning of the twentieth century, therefore, Whitehead was rejecting both the Anglican heritage of his youth and the strictures of Euclidian geometry.[28] This tendency to undermine systems of orthodoxy, and introduce heretical readings, was becoming characteristic of his work. Euclid and the Church were rejected; new dimensions of life welcomed Whitehead into the twentieth century.

The Whiteheads moved from Cambridge to London in 1910, where Whitehead would work first for University College London, then as a professor at Imperial College. His position at Imperial began the year the Great War broke out – a war that would affect his agnostic outlook and trigger his focussed philosophical pursuit. On 13th March 1918, eight months before the end of the War, Whitehead's son Eric, a pilot for the Royal Flying Corps, was killed in action at a mere nineteen years of age. When Whitehead heard of Eric's death his immediate response was 'a sickly smile'.[29] His extended response, however, was philosophy. In his 'Autobiographical Notes', he writes that 'his philosophic writings started in London, at the latter end of the war'.[30] Russell commented that the 'pain of this loss had a great deal to do with his turning his thoughts to philosophy and with causing him to seek ways of escaping from belief in a merely mechanistic universe.'[31] Immanent to his emerging philosophy that sought to augment mechanistic causes with purposes, final causes, was an intertwined theistic streak, a return to religion. Both of Whitehead's other children, North and Jessie, attributed this return to the death of their younger brother.[32] One must, however, be cautious of attributing, to this theistic return, too large a degree of influence to Eric's death – it is an unknown, even to Whitehead himself, one might speculate, and his later 'religion' is hardly consoling, as we shall discover. Moreover, attributing a psychological reason for a philosophic position does not *per se* invalidate the objectivity of that position (such an accusation would be to commit the genetic fallacy). Whitehead's first book after the War, *An Enquiry Concerning the Principles of Knowledge* (1919), was, however, dedicated to his son: 'The music of his life was without discord, perfect in its beauty.'

Whitehead's period of agnosticism spanned Eric's two decades of life. Before this period Whitehead was Anglican, afterwards his theism gradually re-emerged, but not in any orthodox manner. It does appear, though, that Whitehead's agnosticism was always strained as it was a rejection of his inherited English[33] and family identity, and of his deeper feelings. His son, North, considered his father's agnosticism odd, 'like that of a priest celebrating Black Mass'.[34] Russell wrote of Whitehead that 'something of the vicarage atmosphere remained in his ways of feeling and came out in his later philosophical writings'.[35] Yet the Anglicanism of the vicarage and the belief in its God never returned – Whitehead was to reform theology through philosophy. This escape from Anglicanism and agnosticism was reflected in his abandonment of England for the United States in 1924, where he took the position of Professor of Philosophy at Harvard University. It is here where his metaphysics fully developed. He died in Cambridge, Massachusetts, in 1947. Whitehead would supersede the orthodoxy of his biological forefathers by adopting and amending the heterodoxy of his spiritual forefathers, *the metaphysicians* – notably Spinoza and Leibniz. To this new, heretical understanding of religion we now turn.

Part II: Cosmology

Plato argued that body and soul were separate substances,[36] and this dualist legacy has heavily influenced Christianity – even if it be not scriptural or of creed[37] – by inspiring a belief in the survival of the *soul* after bodily destruction. In the Modern Age, Descartes stated that the purpose of his arguments for the separation of the soul and body was to fulfil this exposition as ordained by Pope Leo X.[38] Descartes – a mathematician and philosopher like Whitehead – bifurcated nature into mind and matter, and only human mind at that. Matter, *res extensa*, had the sole essential quality of extension, space. Mind, *res cogitans*, was not considered spatial, extended, and so was deemed a separate substance. These two substances, Descartes argued, interacted at the pineal gland in the brain – but how such interaction was possible he could never adequately explain. As the age of the machine approached, the natural philosophy of the West came to discard the notion of the mind, or soul, as a separate substance. Yet it held unwittingly on to the belief – advanced by Descartes – that 'matter' was devoid of mind or of sentience in any sense. That matter was merely mechanical and mathematically comprehendible was a position congruent with both dualistic Christianity and scientific, mechanistic thinking. But, inveighs Whitehead: 'The disastrous separation of body and mind which has been fixed on European thought by Descartes is responsible for this blindness of science.'[39]

Whitehead's protestations against both religion and science stem from the same philosophic, *dualist* source. The heresy levelled at Bruno and Spinoza was in part due to their *monist* conflation of mind and matter.[40] Bruno was burnt at the stake in 1600 by the Roman Inquisition, and Spinoza was excommunicated by his Sephardic Jewish community, and then reprimanded by the Dutch State and its Christian community, primarily for the dissenting argument that God *is* Nature,[41] a *single* substance which from one perspective is seen as matter and from another as mind. Centuries after Spinoza's death (in 1677) it was still hazardous to profess oneself sympathetic to Spinozism[42] – God and Nature, soul and body, could not be tolerated as identical. Saving one's soul in godliness would be impossible if godliness, worldliness, and soul were of one substance: *monism*. Mind-matter separation, substance *dualism*, seemed to theoretically work well for both Church and Industry: without inherent sentience, nature was a lifeless commodity with no intrinsic value, to be exploited without qualm – the focus could therefore be on saving the human soul and on extending capital and territory.

By striking at this philosophic dualism, the common source of religion and science, Whitehead alters both to inaugurate a potential New Reformation of Western creed. That philosophy, science, and religion are considered as separate disciplines is itself a failure of systematic thought. Let us examine this attack on the common source so to find ourselves in a new world. In his Sixth Meditation of 1641, Descartes writes:

> [B]ecause, on the one side, I have a clear and distinct idea of myself inasmuch as I am only a thinking and unextended thing, and as, on the other, I possess a distinct idea of body, inasmuch

> as it is only and extended and unthinking thing, it is certain that this I [the soul] is entirely and absolutely distinct from my body, and can exist without it.[43]

In essence, Descartes' argument is that because mind (the soul) *appears* to have very different qualities to matter (the body) – e.g. an emotion appears to have no material length and weight – then mind and matter must actually *be* distinct, as one has clear and distinct, thus *adequate*, ideas of both. The heaving meat of the body *appears* to be completely distinct from the lofty thoughts of the mind, and so Descartes argued that this appearance reflected reality: they actually *were* distinct. It is this Cartesian epistemological-to-ontological inference that Whitehead dismisses. That one perceives and conceives matter and mind as having distinct properties does not, in fact, entail that matter and mind *are* distinct. Whitehead argues, in Bergsonian fashion,[44] that our perception and conception, our view of the world, is very limited and consequently *does not adequately* provide us with the full, concrete nature of the object observed. Whitehead writes that, 'sense-perception omits any discrimination of the fundamental activities within nature. For example, consider the difference between the paving stone as perceived visually … [and] the paving stone as described by the physicist'.[45] When we consider the fact that we only perceive a *fragment* of that which we conceive as a 'paving-stone' – we do not perceive the other side of the stone, let alone its inner busy constellation of particles – then we realize that our perception, and the conception related thereto, gives us *abstraction rather than adequacy*, contra Descartes. We cannot trust that the ways things appear reflect the way they actually are. Perceptions and conceptions give us abstractions only. An abstraction is *part of* a concrete, adequate, truth – it is an extract from the whole. To mistake an abstraction for a concrete truth is an all-too-common human error that Whitehead names the *Fallacy of Misplaced Concreteness*.[46]

Whitehead advances this insight to say that our knowledge of 'matter' itself is far from adequate. This is meant not only in the sense of 'pessimistic induction'[47] – that we cannot be satisfied with current scientific understandings as they are constantly changing throughout history – but more profoundly, that 'matter' includes qualities that we might call mental,[48] such as primal, basic forms of will and memory. This is a form of *panpsychism*, more specifically referred to as *panexperientialism* or *pan-valuism*.[49] In the mid twentieth century, when philosophy and science were at their most austere and mechanical state with regard to the utter reduction of mind to matter, the panpsychism of Whitehead – 'the most distinguished champion of panpsychism in the twentieth century'[50] – was heresy, punishable by spurn and disregard. The orthodox view, explicit in philosophy, implicit in science, was that of *materialism*: that the fundamentally real stuff of nature was physical matter. Mind was considered merely an offshoot of certain configurations of such matter, viz. the configuration of *parts of the brain only* (not of *all matter*, as in panpsychism). In an influential[51] 1959 essay, philosopher J.J.C. Smart, for instance, writes that: 'Man himself will one day be explicable in mechanistic terms. … [This] is largely a confession of *faith*'.[52] It was such an orthodox faith in materialism that Whitehead shunned, and he was shunned in return. The workings of faith are not limited to religion; the orthodoxy excommunicated the heretic. The legacy of such heresy can be summarized with a remark from contemporary philosopher Pierfrancesco Basile: 'Among the truly outstanding philosophers of the twentieth century, Alfred North Whitehead holds the unenviable status of being the most neglected.'[53]

What were Whitehead's reasons for holding such a panpsychological heresy – one that was heretical not only to Church, but also to twentieth-century science and philosophy? To elucidate the reasoning behind this abstraction-derived panpsychism, consider the following. When one looks at another person, one *sees* only a fragment of what they concretely *are*. One may augment the seeing with hearing, smelling, tasting, and touching, yet the perception these traditional senses provide excludes fundamental aspects of that other. The other person's own conscious states, such as his vision, his thoughts, are not perceived by another.

One can *infer* such conscious states in the other, but this is *inference rather than observation*. We know, therefore, that in beings such as ourselves, our perception of another body is *inadequate* in providing comprehensive knowledge of that body. We consequently have no rational prerogative to believe that our perception, using our senses or the latest scientific apparatus, gives us adequate, sufficient, knowledge of body, or matter, more generally. A microscope or brain scan will never perceive another's perspective, just as a thermometer will never perceive an object's colour. The retort against panpsychism that a *brain* is necessary for primal mentality is likewise a claim that cannot be based on observation – it is faith not science. How could one observe that *intelligently behaved yet brainless* starfish or plants, say, have no sentience? That nature, furthermore, is not fundamentally one with humanity in its intrinsic sentient qualities is an anthropocentrism not yet made widely apparent.[54] It is this accusation of science itself being unscientific and faith-based in its assumptions that places Whitehead as the prime heretic of the scientific age, but in the progressive sense in which Galileo is retrospectively viewed, in his heliocentric heresy. Scientific heresy need not be rejection of science.

We cannot therefore know that mind and matter are fundamentally distinct, as Descartes argued, based on our perceptions and the concepts based thereupon. Clear and distinct ideas are not enough to assert concrete knowledge. Moreover, Whitehead adds, we should not believe that our perception is limited to the traditional five senses. Both matter and perception are not as limited as we conceive. In addition to traditional sensation, which Whitehead calls Perception in the Mode of Presentational Immediacy, there is Perception in the Mode of Causal Efficiency. The latter is a 'primitive form of physical experience'[55] which involves the *actual absorption* of part of the perceived object and of the subject's own past into the ever-renewing process that is the subject. It is a form of perception primitive to all entities, even though its reality for us has been masked by the former, presentational type of perception. As mentality is ubiquitous in matter as intrinsic quality, the nature of

Perception in the Mode of Causal Efficiency is sentient, as a vague, yet aesthetically valuable, 'blind emotion'.[56] *Causation here is perception*; there is no direct causation without perception in the universe, all forces are felt, *absorption is causation which is perception*. This primal perception is difficult to become conscious of, though certain sensitive poets have expressed it. Whitehead commends Wordsworth for such conveyance, especially in *The Prelude*.[57]

Such primitive perception of the intrinsic quality of nature is not a perception registered by current science. Whitehead laments that,

> [S]cience as conceived as resting on mere sense-perception, with no other source of observation, is bankrupt .... Science can find no individual enjoyment in nature: Science can find no aim in nature: Science can find no creativity in nature; it finds mere rules of succession .... The reason for this blindness of Physical Science lies in the fact that such Science only deals with half the evidence provided by human experience.[58]

Modern science, philosophy, and religion, have committed – unwittingly or no – the fallacy of misplaced concreteness by taking the traditional abstractions 'matter' and 'perception' for concrete realities, a mistake which has led to the two errors of believing either that mind and matter are separate (dualism), or of believing that mind is reducible to matter (materialism). Both lead to the intractable 'hard problem of consciousness':[59] the supposed mystery as to how mind and matter relate. Materialism is in truth also, paradoxically, a dualism because it separates mind as something distinct from matter, as *something* which can then be 'reduced' to matter, be it in terms of emergence, illusion, or psychoneural identity.

Whitehead's analysis of experience not only reveals the limitations (and therefore possibilities) for current science, it also reveals the limitations and possibilities for religion. Whitehead sees both science and religion as open to development. Temporary forms, such as Newtonianism and Anglicanism, are but passing skins to be shed, parts of a process that need never end.

Complementing our additional primitive perception, Whitehead proceeds, are more exalted forms of experience. Prosaic consciousness is but common, not comprehensive, sentience: there are the primal forms below, and the Elysian forms above. These exalted forms include the cosmic, mystical experiences that seemingly accompany every human epoch, as elaborated by cognoscenti such as Richard M. Bucke and William James.[60] For Whitehead, religion comes from the individual religious experience rather than from social structures,

> Religion is the art and the theory of the internal life of man ... . This doctrine is the direct negation of the theory that religion is primarily a social fact. ... Religion is what the individual does with his own solitariness. ... Collective enthusiasms, revivals, institutions, churches, rituals, bibles, codes of behaviour, are the trappings of religion, its passing forms.[61]

In a recently discovered essay by Whitehead called 'The Religious Psychology of the Western Peoples', much is levelled against these passing forms of religion. Against the dogmatists and Inquisitors, he writes that it 'was assumed that God preferred exact verbal expression to loving kindness'.[62] In *Adventures of Ideas* he is more specific, attacking his own former forms: 'the later Protestant Reformation was ... [a] complete failure, in no way improving Catholic theology'.[63] In the same book he is also more general: '[The] true enemy [is] the doctrine of dogmatic finality, a doctrine which flourished and is flourishing with equal vigour throughout Theology, Science, and Metaphysics.'[64] This statement of solidarity with all heretics against dogmatists is complemented by the oft-quoted line that prefaces his metaphysical magnum opus, *Process and Reality*: 'In philosophical discussion, the merest hint of dogmatic certainty as to finality of statement is an exhibition of folly.'[65] In this respect, heresy is a fundamental function of philosophy and theology, orthodoxy a symptom of decay.

Religion as social dogma is not true religion. What then does Whitehead consider to be true religion, freed from its social cage? In *Science and the Modern World* he writes:

> [R]eligion is the expression of one type of fundamental experiences of mankind .... The insistence upon rules of conduct [merely] marks the ebb of religious fervour. ... Religion is the vision of something which stands beyond, behind, and within, the passing flux of immediate things; something which is real, and yet waiting to be realised; something which is a remote possibility, and yet the greatest of present facts; something that gives meaning to all that passes, and yet eludes apprehension; something whose possession is the final good, and yet is beyond all reach; something which is the ultimate ideal, and the hopeless quest.[66]

Religion, like science, is an ongoing creative process of exploration – both err but both evolve. By abstracting from the full range of experience only that which can be metrically quantified and reifying it into a presumed concrete actuality, human thought has erred into religious and scientific stagnation and dogma. By expanding the analysis of experience and taking that expansion as equally veracious to prosaic experience, Whitehead transgresses Western thought through a super-empiricism conducive to a systematic metaphysics. There is sentience below, in all things, and a sentience above, a God, and above it, a cosmic, creative advance. Somewhat reminiscent of Bruno and Spinoza's God, Whitehead's God is interlaced within all entities, as we shall see. Whitehead's theology is thus a form of pantheism, fused with his panpsychism.

Though critical of Christian dogma and denominations, Whitehead at times expresses sympathy for Christ's message of love, and the canonical Gospels against the abrasiveness of the Pauline Epistles in the New Testament.[67] These Christian sympathies were no doubt formative in the American theological interpretation of Whitehead's thought as 'process theology'. But in truth these expressed sympathies betrayed only the particular affinities of the 'vicarage atmosphere' of his youth, his Anglican upbringing and study. In its essence, Whitehead's religion of a pantheo-panpsychism, not to mention the aesthetic drive of his God (as indicated below), has little affinity with Christianity.[68] Whitehead was religious but he was not a Christian, his religious vision was even meta-theistic: God is not the highest principle of religion.[69] Whitehead's God, moreover, can in some aspects be seen as anti-Christian and more pagan in its valuation of Nature in Herself.

Pierfrancesco Basile describes 'Whitehead's theory of a primarily egoistic God ... [as] morally repulsive'.[70] Victor Lowe conveyed that Whitehead's God was seen as 'an aesthete of highly dubious moral character, not worthy of being called God.'[71] Indeed, Whitehead's God is neither based on nor congruent with morality or scripture, but with metaphysical necessity. In this respect, and in the 'egoistic' nature of his God, Whitehead's cold theism is reminiscent of Aristotle's pagan deity:[72] 'In the place of Aristotle's Prime Mover, we require God as the Principle of Concretion.'[73] That is, in order to explain concrete actuality one must invoke God. Let us examine the reasons for the invocation of such a heathen divinity, antagonistic in its very essence to modern orthodoxy: Christian, philosophic, and scientific.

As we saw, anterior to complex forms of conscious experience there is the primal form of perception in the mode of causal efficacy. This is a fundamental form of perception ubiquitous in nature, from man to molecule, and below that still. Whitehead names the most primal entities of reality 'actual occasions', or 'actual entities'. An electron is a 'society' of such actual occasions, which are also referred to, in Jamesian manner,[74] as *drops of experience*. An actual entity is a process that 'prehends' – that is, perceives in the mode of causal efficacy – other actual entities that thereby enter into that prehending actual entity so as to constitute it. But this perception has a dipolar nature: an actual entity physically prehends other actual entities, but it also conceptually perceives 'eternal objects'. These are Whitehead's variant of what are traditionally referred to as *universals*. Universals dress other entities with a certain appearance. For instance, to take a human example, I may see an actual apple as *green*. The actual apple has a physical, finite existence, but the colour of it does not perish with it. A colour has a type of existence beyond each of its instantiations. The colour green, for instance, was not born nor will it die[75] – it is timeless, eternal: an eternal object of cognition. As well as colours and other qualia, eternal objects include abstract objects such as mathematical theorems, many of which have an existence though they have not yet been discovered or realized in our world. Indeed, eternal objects exist, or subsist, in another world, 'the realm of eternality'.[76] Whitehead also names these eternal objects 'potentialities', therefore we have two modes of existence: actuality and potentiality.[77] This realm of potentiality, of eternal objects, is one of the two aspects of God: 'the primordial nature of God'.[78]

An actual entity thus requires this primordial aspect of God for the process of self-creation that Whitehead calls 'concrescence'. Each actual entity has the purpose of achieving its self-creation, which in its completion is the achievement, or satisfaction, of *value*. This aimed-for achievement which completes the concrescence of an actual entity is the final cause, *telos*, of each such occasion. Consequently, *teleology* is reintroduced into cosmology, contrary to the scientific outlook of the age which considers final causation to be non-extant, since commonly understood 'perception' can only disclose efficient, physical causation. But Whitehead is not apologetic: 'A satisfactory cosmology must explain the interweaving of efficient and of final causation.'[79] The very existence of reason cannot be explained without the involvement of final causation, he writes, because our purposeful, conscious intellectual efforts would be without any efficacy if all actions were caused solely by unconscious mechanical, efficient causes. That is, reason would have *no power* at all if it could be reduced to mechanical, efficient causation. And if there were no reason for reason, reason would not have evolved: 'In the course of evolution why should the trend have arrived at mankind, if his activities of Reason remain without influence on his bodily actions?'[80] Reason does exist, and as a consequence so does purposeful efficacy, teleology. Science is blind to that which conditions it, an oddity of the current age that triggers Whitehead's observation that, 'Scientists animated by the purpose of proving that they are purposeless constitute an interesting subject for study.'[81] Such obvious absurdities betray the limited scope of the current scientific method.

The second aspect of God, 'the consequent nature of God', is not transcendent but immanent: each actual occasion's achievement of value is felt by God and becomes eternally part of God. He is therefore 'the fellow-sufferer who understands'.[82] Even the experience of suffering is a form of value as it is an intensity of experience. Moreover, and more darkly, God's,

> aim for [actual occasions] is depth of satisfaction as an intermediate step towards the fulfilment of his own being .... Thus God's purpose in the creative advance is the evocation of intensities. The evocation of societies [higher organisms] is purely subsidiary to this absolute end.[83]

Here we begin to see the narcissism, perhaps the hedonism, of God in Whitehead. God's aim transcending ours is aesthetic harmony. Consequently, for Whitehead, 'evil' is fragmentation of purpose inducive to harmony. But there is a cacophony of harmonies, and thus values are relative to each harmony. There are harmonies in morality, logic, religion, and art, none of which take objective precedence as to importance.[84] Contrary to religious doctrines prescribing conduct, Whitehead writes:

> morality does not indicate what you are to do in mythological abstractions. It does concern the general ideal which should be the justification for any particular objective. The destruction of man, or of an insect, or of a tree, or of the Parthenon, may be moral or immoral.[85]

Whitehead, naturally, has his own subjective, personal ideals that constitute his ideal harmony, the potential fragmentations of which he considers 'evils'. These 'evils', however, are then, subjective not objective. Subjective to both himself and the culture from which he expresses them. He lists some of these as: 'the loss of religious faith, the malignant use of material power, the degradation attending a differential birth rate favouring the lower types of humanity, [and] the suppression of aesthetic creativeness'.[86] Some of these may be anathema to today's 'evils', but there is no absolute standard of moral objectivity for Whitehead that could judge them as right or wrong. That would require, as Nietzsche emphasizes, a God as absolute judge and ideal. That such a God is dead, along with its slave morality, is a belief shared by both Nietzsche and Whitehead. It was in fact the latter who wrote that '[u]nfortunately ... there has survived throughout history the older concept of a Divine Despot and a slavish Universe, each with the morals of its kind.'[87] Such subtle subversions of morality mark Whitehead out as heretical also to the 'secular religions', the moral ideologies that swither and sway throughout the modern mind without anchor.

Whitehead's God neither gives us morality nor does He provide the ultimate ground of reality. God itself is an actual entity 'in the grip of the ultimate metaphysical ground, the creative advance into novelty'.[88] The religious vision quoted above can transcend God – this is the meta-theism as mysticism. Contrary to the Abrahamic religions, God is not omnipotent, omniscient, nor omnibenevolent. He is a unique actual entity, but He is not supreme.

It is creativity into novelty that is the fundamental process of reality. Whitehead calls his process philosophy 'the philosophy of organism' because actual entities, and 'societies' thereof, are sentient organisms that, as such, evolve. The organic-inorganic dichotomy is merely linguistic rather than real: all actuality is fundamentally organic in its units. These units are analogous to Leibniz's monads, though Whitehead's notion of 'prehension' provides windows for each unit, entity, organism, to actually interact (in contrast to Leibniz's isolationist monadology).[89] The so-called 'laws of nature' are mere abstractions that reflect the regular character of such entities over a prolonged period. As material 'particles' are but societies of such entities, *matter itself evolves along with the 'laws of nature'*. Such evolution cannot be determined because determination would be based upon the assumption that 'laws' were constant and themselves not subject to process. Entities are determined in part not by 'laws', but by their immediate precursors – the actual entities from which they stem – and by the eternal objects that ingress into them. But this determination is not complete: novel eternal objects are always potentially manifested. Contrary to the modern monolithic thought of physics, Whitehead affirms that a 'type of [cosmic] order decays; not into disorder, but by passing into a new type of order. That is my answer with respect to the question of entropy'.[90] At his seventieth birthday celebration at the Harvard Club in Boston, he harks back to his first mathematical forays with Grassmann et al. in his appraisal of the contemporary situation:

> our epoch illustrates one special type of order. For example, this absurdly limited number of three dimensions of space is a sign that you have got something characteristic of a special order. ... [Yet there are] other types of order of which you and I have not the faintest notion, unless perchance they are to be found in our highest mentality and are unperceived by us in their true relevance to the future. ... [The] universe [is] always driving on to novelty.[91]

Contrary to modern, static substance-based philosophy and science, Whitehead advances a process philosophy of organism where even matter, space-time, and the laws of nature are, in Heraclitean fashion, in a state of flux. Organisms evolve, and all actuality is organism. Contrary to modern religion and its moral legacy, Whitehead affirms an aesthete God who is also immersed in the flux of actuality, and a morality not statically tied to absolute ideals but it too subject to processual change. The creative advance is an unforgiving torrent.

Closing Remarks

If the 'European philosophical tradition ... consists of a series of footnotes to Plato',[92] then Western philosophy begins with heresy: the inquisition and fatal poisoning of Plato's teacher, Socrates.[93] Though such punishment for allegedly questioning the gods might have made Plato sympathetic to religious dissent, the contrary occurred. Plato, as we saw, came to prescribe imprisonment and death for heresy.[94] When Whitehead speaks of Plato it is mostly with utmost praise, but in this case Whitehead is unrepentant: 'Plato is the originator of the heresies and the feeblest side of Christian Theology.'[95] This origination largely flowed through the conduit of St Augustine of Hippo, whose 'final influence for posterity was on the side of a narrow orthodoxy and the forcible suppression of heretics. He approved of their execution'.[96] It was the realization of such an intolerant legacy that aided Whitehead's escape from the Church. But his feelings, experience, and reason led him back to a *greater* religious vision: of an eccentric, aesthete God overpowered by the creative advance of the universe. This outlook was fostered by his analysis of the nature of experience, an analysis that led him away from the orthodoxies of science and philosophy in their misplaced reifications. Whitehead was neither given hemlock nor burnt at the stake for such serious dissent, but his philosophy was largely disregarded[97] by the scientific and philosophic establishment, the latter of which had, Whitehead opined in 1936, 'gone dry'[98] in Europe. At this time, in Whitehead's homeland, Wittgenstein was teaching at Cambridge University, and Gilbert Ryle was teaching at Oxford. Their influence desiccated the interest in deeper philosophy. Whitehead's grand metaphysics 'was ignored, rather than rejected on philosophical grounds'[99] because his attack on the aforementioned presumptions of religion, science, and philosophy ran counter to the general interests of the post-war West. Religion was stagnant, science was advancing blindly, and philosophy had become the dogsbody of science, replacing metaphysics with mere linguistic and syllogistic analysis. Whitehead's thought was discordant with the times, but in accord with the greater creative impulse of the cosmos – this systematic concrescence of dissent marked him out as the arch-heretic of prevalent ideology.

— — —

Acknowledgements

I thank Karina Jakubowicz and Robert Dickins for their helpful editing of this piece, a chapter which first appeared in their 2021 edited volume *Heresy and Borders in the Twentieth Century* (London: Routledge).

Notes

1. Trinity College, Cambridge.
2. "heresy, n.". OED Online. June 2020. Oxford University Press. Accessed on 28 July 2020: https://www.oed.com/view/Entry/86195?redirectedFrom=heresy
3. Plato, 2016, p.400, (909d).
4. 'Orthodox' is a word that comes from the Greek ὀρθοδοξία, meaning *right opinion*.
5. This tract is from 'The New Forcers of Conscience' (1646) – Qtd. in Gregory, 2013, p. 149.
6. Lowe, 1990, p. 194.
7. A 'Tractarian' was one sympathetic to the tracts written by members of the Oxford Movement, as described below. An 'Ecumenical' was a Christian who sought co-operation and unity between the various Christian denominations.
8. Whitehead, 1941, pp. 3.
9. Russell, 1967/8/9/1991, p. 130.
10. Russell, 1958, p. 94.
11. Price, 1954, p. 361.
12. Lowe, 1985, p. 44.
13. Ollard and Crosse, 1912, p. 390.
14. Whitehead's biographer, Victor Lowe, claims that his agnosticism began in either 1897 or 1898: Lowe, 1985, p. 188.
15. Price, 1954, p. 234.
16. Ibid., p. 235 (recorded as being said on 19 June 1943).
17. Before the Minkowski-Einsteinian replacement theory came (in 1905), physicists had already realized that the Newtonian edifice was collapsing. Before Einstein's mathematics teacher Minkowski had suggested that time be a fourth dimension of space, this general idea had already been presented in the fiction of the time: in Wells, H.G. (1895) *The Time Machine*. London: William Heinemann.
18. Palmer, 1845, p. 331.

19   See Collum, 1977, p. 16; Gilbert, 1980, pp. 71–6. Whitehead was not a member of the Conservative party, but was supportive of the opposing Liberal Party of the time.

20   The slight English aversion to these two figures might be epitomized through Russell's contention that 'I should regard Socialism in its milder forms as a natural development of the Christian tradition. But Marx belongs with Nietzsche as an apostle of disruption...' – Russell, 1991, p. 495, in a letter dated 18 June 1941 to Gilbert Murray.

21   Whitehead, 1941, pp. 5–6.

22   Qtd. in Lowe, 1985, pp. 114–5.

23   In the words of the atheist Arthur Schopenhauer, 'Philosophy has the peculiarity of presupposing absolutely nothing as known; everything to it is equally strange and a problem.' Schopenhauer, 1818/1969, p. 81.

24   Whitehead, 1929, p. 30.

25   Other notable Apostles of the time included Virginia Woolf's older cousin, the poet J.K. Stephen, the Bloomsbury Group founder Lytton Strachey, philosopher G.E. Moore, mathematician W.K. Clifford, author Walter Raleigh; later notable Apostles included E.M. Forster, John Maynard Keynes, Ludwig Wittgenstein, Henry Jackson, G.H. Hardy; earlier notables included Alfred Tennyson, F.D. Maurice, Erasmus Alvey Darwin (his brother Charles Darwin was not admitted), and James Clerk Maxwell, to list but a fragment.

26   These questions and answers were noted in the Society's records and disclosed to Whitehead's biographer Victor Lowe by the Apostle and philosopher Prof. R. B. Braithwaite – see Chapter VII of Lowe, 1985.

27   William Kingdon Clifford (1845–79), also a Cambridge Apostle, though one whom Whitehead never met in person, was more influential than Whitehead in terms of developing geometries of spaces of more than three dimensions, especially in applications to both force and feeling. See Clifford, 1904, and the chapter Deeper than Depth, §3:v, in this volume.

28   At least in the transgressing of Euclid's fifth postulate: that parallel lines never meet.

29   This response was reported to Victor Lowe by Eric's brother North: Lowe, 1990, p. 34.

30   Whitehead, 1941, p. 13.

31   Russell, 1958, p. 95. Russell also rejected such mechanistic thought.

32   They conveyed this to Victor Lowe in 1967 and 1972, respectively: Lowe, 1990, pp. 188 and 362.

33   Anglicanism and being English were interwoven identities – see Collum, 1977, p. 15ff.

34   This he said to Victor Lowe: Lowe, 1985, p. 190.

35   Russell, 1958, p. 97.

36   As argued, for instance, in *The Phaedo* and *The Republic*: Plato, 1956.

37 See Keenan, 1996, pp. 33–45, for the rejection of substance dualism as Christian; see Mounce, 2010, pp. 401–407, for the opposing view.
38 Descartes, 1996, p. 51. Leo X was the Pope whose Indulgences Luther famously protested.
39 Whitehead, 1938/1958, p. 211.
40 Giordano Bruno's monism is expressed notably in the Fifth Dialogue of: *Cause, Principle and Unity*, 1584/1998.
41 This is best argued in his great work, *Ethics*, 1677/1991.
42 Consider the so-called 'Pantheism Controversy', or the fact that Spinoza inaugurated the aforementioned 'higher criticism' of the Bible in his *Theological-Political Treatise* (1670/2001).
43 Descartes, 1996, p. 100.
44 Bergson, H. (1907/1998). Ch. 1.
45 Whitehead, 1938/1958, p. 210.
46 Whitehead, 1925/1967, p. 51ff.
47 Laudan, 1981, pp. 19–49.
48 The 'mental' used here does not of necessity include the high-grade consciousness of humans. Human consciousness to primal mentality is analogous to the complexity of a human body as compared to an atom.
49 David R. Griffin coined the term *panexperientialism* for Whitehead's strand: Cobb and Griffin, 1977), pt.3, ch.4; Victor Lowe coined the term *pan-valuism*, Lowe, 1990, pp.168 and 270.
50 Edwards, 1967, p. 31.
51 Jaegwon Kim writes that '"Sensations and Brain Processes" had a critical role in establishing the psychoneural identity theory as a major position on the mind-body problem': Kim, 2011, p. 98.
52 Smart, 1959, pp. 142–3. (My italics.)
53 Basile, 2017/8, p. vii.
54 In the first part of the twenty-first century, panpsychism has become more popular – with arguments issuing from high-profile philosophers such as Galen Strawson, Thomas Nagel, and David Chalmers. See for instance the edited collection, from Brüntrup and Jaskolla, 2017.
55 Whitehead, 1929/1985, p. 162.
56 Ibid.
57 Whitehead, 1925/1967, pp. 83–4 (ch. V).
58 Whitehead, 1938/1958, p. 211.
59 Chalmers, D. J. (1995). 'Facing up to the Problem of Consciousness' in *Journal of Consciousness Studies,*: Vol.2, No.3, pp. 200–219.
60 See Bucke, 1901/1947; James, 1902/1985; James, 1910, pp. 85–92.

61 Whitehead, 1927/2011, pp. 6–7.
62 Whitehead, A.N. (n.d.) 'Religious Psychology of the Western Peoples', p.16, ADD020, *Whitehead Research Library*: http://wrl.whiteheadresearch.org/items/show/1414 .
63 Whitehead, 1933/1967, p. 166. Whitehead came to prefer Roman Catholicism to Protestantism partly because of its greater aesthetic appeal.
64 Ibid., p. 162.
65 Whitehead, 1929/1985, p. xiv.
66 Whitehead, 1925/1967, pp. 191–2.
67 Whitehead, 1927/2011, p. 64.
68 I have made this case in the chapter, The Great God Pan is Not Dead – in this volume.
69 The religious vision quoted above is of more than God: it includes the creative advance too.
70 Basile, 2017/8, p. 110.
71 Lowe, 1990, p. 199.
72 See Whitehead, 1925/1967, p. 173.
73 Ibid., p. 174.
74 James, 1909/1920, p. 232ff. James himself is inspired in this later work by Hegel, Fechner, and Bergson.
75 Whitehead, 1925/1967, p. 86ff.
76 Ibid., p. 176.
77 On these two worlds, see his late essay, 'Immortality' in Schilpp, 1941, pp. 682–700.
78 Whitehead, 1929/1985, p. 343ff.
79 Whitehead, 1929, p. 22.
80 Ibid. Note that this evolutionary argument against epiphenomenalism is also advanced by William James, F. H. Bradley and Karl Popper.
81 Ibid., p. 12.
82 Whitehead, 1929/1985, p. 351.
83 Ibid., p. 105.
84 'The terms morality, logic, religion, art, have each of them been claimed as exhausting the whole meaning of importance. Each of them denotes a subordinate species. But the genus stretches beyond any finite group of species.' Whitehead, 1938/1958, p. 16.
85 Ibid., p. 20. See also Whitehead 1933/1967, p. 291.
86 Whitehead, 1925/1967, p. 204.
87 Whitehead, 1933/1967, p. 26. See also p. 290 (ch. 20).
88 Whitehead, 1929/1985, p. 349.

89	See especially Leibniz's essays 'Discourse on Metaphysics' (1686), 'New System of Nature' (1695), and 'The Principles of Philosophy, or, the Monadology' (1714) in Leibniz, 1989. Leibniz kept the first unpublished as it was considered by a confidante as heretical.
90	Whitehead, 1961, p. 219. This is from a lecture given at Whitehead's seventieth birthday celebration at the Harvard Club in Boston, 1931.
91	Ibid., p. 220.
92	Whitehead, 11929/1985, p. 39.
93	See Socrates' trial in Plato's *Apology* (Plato, 1956, pp. 57–88). Western philosophy's heretical start predates that of the heretical start of its religion: Socrates is a precursor to Jesus Christ.
94	Plato, 2016, pp. 394ff (904d, 907d–908b, 909d–e, 910c). Plato only allows for the discussion of religious orthodoxy by a group of learned men in secrecy, reminiscent of that enacted by the Cambridge Apostles.
95	Whitehead, 1933/1967, p. 167.
96	Whitehead, (n. d.: 'Religious Psychology of the Western Peoples'), p. 18.
97	Whitehead did, however, inspire the formation of epigenetics through C. H. Waddington.
98	Letter to Charles Hartshorne, 2 January 1936 (Lowe, 1990, p. 345). Whitehead wrote that 'America will be the centre of worthwhile philosophy', citing William James and Charles Peirce.
99	Basile, 2017/8, p. vii.

IV
Psychedelic Experience
Revelation, Hallucination, or Otherwise?

Vast varieties of experiences can be occasioned by psychedelic substances, from the mundane or irritating, to the sublime, world-destroying, world-creating. Under the influence we seemingly encounter alien states of mind, and alien worlds – the mysterious subjective and the mystery of the objective: Can psychedelic states reveal any objective reality or are they always subjective? For some explorers, there is a 'noetic' aspect to certain psychedelic states: a feeling that one has undergone, as William James puts it, 'states of insight into depths of truth unplumbed by the discursive intellect. They are illuminations, revelations'.[1] The feeling of obtaining novel knowledge concerning fundamental reality is often accompanied by correlated qualms. In the words of Nobel laureate Octavio Paz, 'The person who takes a [psychedelic] drug implicitly doubts the solidity of reality – he is not sure that it is what it appears to be and what our instruments define it as being, or he suspects that another reality exists.'[2]

For some psychonauts, such noetic feeling suffices for full-on belief in the objective existence (the *veridicality*) of the apparent realities perceived. Such apparent realities may involve fearful four-dimensional praying mantis machines, fiendish pixies pursuing some vital interstellar factory logistics, or one's becoming a sentient polyhedron, eternally spinning for the sake of love. William James, however, reserves noeticism more for the grander metaphysical schemes such as belief in the unreality of time or space, the unity of subject and its object, moreover the ultimate unity of all things, the ubiquity of minds in all entities or mind in all entities (panpsychism and pantheism, respectively), and an intuition of intrinsic values embedded within Nature.

For others, such so-called psychedelically-induced mysticism[3] yields no insight into reality at all. Such rejection comes in two main, albeit contrary, strands: the theist and the physicalist. Certain theistic thinkers[4] consider induced mysticism to be, as it were, fake mysticism, revealing no truth in comparison to the revelations of the ordained saints and established mystics. On the other side, the physicalist, or materialist, also takes induced mysticism to be non-revelatory and thus merely subjective. That which the physicalist and the theistic, religious sceptic share is the belief that the existence of a physical substance (the drug) and its neurological ramifications (the neural correlates of psychedelic consciousness) is a *sufficient condition* for explaining the psychedelic experience. Here there is no need to involve the divine or the *meta*physical as a *cause* of a psychedelic experience. Thus the experience is either dismissed as sacrilegious and delusional, or as merely delusional.

But beyond these two extremes – the all-out belief of the mantis-veridicalists and the all-out rejection of the theist-physicalists – there lies the possibility that certain experiences are veridical, others non-veridical: some revelations, others hallucinations. How could this veridicality be determined?

For a *veridical experience* one requires: 1. physiological perceptive processes, such as functioning eyes and brain, and 2. an external perceived object, such as a lamp. Both 1. and 2. (subject and object) are necessary for an experience of the real. Neither is sufficient, i.e. enough, by itself to yield a real, veridical experience. 1. without 2. would be a hallucination; 2. without 1. would not be an experience at all. We see, therefore, that the criterion for determining an experience as hallucinatory is not merely the existence of neural correlates of the experience – we must also rule out the existence of that which is perceived. Consequently, *merely presenting the neural correlates of psychedelic experience does not imply that the experience is non-veridical, hallucinatory*. In likewise fashion, presenting the neural correlates of a perceived lamp does not imply that the lamp is a hallucination. Neural correlates of psychedelic consciousness neither prove nor disprove that which is experienced – they are *not* a sufficient condition for establishing non-veridicality. Neural correlates would be expected for *both* veridical and non-veridical psychedelic experience.

How, then, could we rule out the existence of the external perceived object of a psychedelic experience, as neural correlation alone cannot offer this? There are a number of criteria that generally determine whether what we experience is real or not. These include:[5]

- *Sensibility*: Something sensed by the traditional five senses (sight, sound, etc.) is commonly taken as veridical. Sensibility is useful but not sufficient to give us knowledge of what exists. There are things *that exist of which we can be cognizant* that are not perceived through the traditional senses, such as mathematical theorems and logical axioms. More pertinently, *we cannot even directly perceive the consciousness of others through these senses*. Thus we cannot rule out the existence of objects of psychedelic experiences solely on the basis that they cannot be observed through the traditional senses in prosaic states.
- *Shared objects of experience*: If only I see the lamp, but others do not, I may question the veridicality of my experience. But the experiences of grander psychedelic phenomena listed above –

such as the unity of all, and the unreality of time – are common, shared objects of experience under the psychedelic influence.
- *Coherence with other beliefs*: An object perceived through the senses that does not cohere with one's network of prior beliefs will often be dismissed as unreal. Of course, this is not a strong criterion for veridicality as one's prior beliefs may be false as they are often inculcated rather than developed through reason.
- *Rationality*: If we have background rationale for believing in the veridicality of that which we experience, we are thereby prone to consider the experience as veridical. For example, we may have reasons to doubt the reality of time.[6] Moreover, if we can show that the objects of experience are logically coherent and not contradictory, their veridicality is shown to be possible.

None of these criteria for veridicality refute the veridicality of *all* psychedelic experiences. Yet they neither prove their veridicality. However, the fact that many types of psychedelic experience have *shared objects of experience* – such as the unreality of time, or the unity of subject and object – is suggestive of veridicality. The Cambridge philosopher C. D. Broad argued that, 'So far as [mystical experiences] *agree* they should be provisionally accepted as veridical unless there is some positive ground for thinking that they are not.'[7] The 'positive ground' given by the sceptic theist is that the experiences, (i) are caused by a drug's effects alone, and (ii) do not cohere with their religion. The 'positive ground' of the physicalist is the same (i) as above, and (ii) that they neither cohere with their creed.

We have seen above that (i) is not a positive ground: chemically-induced correlates of mystical experience cannot *per se* disprove the objectivity of that which is experienced. With regard to (ii), let us consider the creed of the physicalist. This creed claims, in brief, that all that fundamentally exists is matter-energy, spacetime, forces of Nature, and laws of Nature. Sometimes its adherents refer to themselves as 'naturalists' and their detractors as 'supernaturalists'. But as contemporary philosopher Galen Strawson notes, 'One can't ... classify anything as supernatural or nonnatural until one has an account of what is natural.'[8] And such physicalism cannot account for that which is most natural to each of us: *consciousness*. Some strands of physicalism believe that consciousness does not exist – but this is a performative contradiction (belief in the unreality of belief). Another strand believes that consciousness *emerges* from matter,[9] but how and by which laws of Nature this occurs is never explained. We must realize that correlation is not explanation. Philosopher of mind Jaegwon Kim reminds us that, '[m]aking a running list of psychoneural correlations does not come anywhere near gaining an explanatory insight into why there are such correlations'.[10] There is no observable causal line between a neuro-physical motion and a conscious emotion. Another strand of physicalism *identifies* mental states with neuro-physical states. But the properties of each type of state are so dissimilar that such identity is rejected on logical grounds. Furthermore, *mental causation* – that a thought or desire can cause a bodily movement or trigger a further mental change – cannot be explained via physicalism yet to deny it would be to render mentality impotent, useless, which would be contrary to both evolutionary[11] and logical principles.[12] These old problems, and others, are encapsulated in the new term, *the hard problem of consciousness*. In truth, *the hard problem of consciousness is a disproof of physicalism*. Physicalism cannot account for consciousness, therefore it cannot be an adequate understanding of reality.[13] Thus the fact that psychedelic experiences do not cohere with the physicalist's view of the world should not lead us to think these experiences are non-veridical.

There appears, then, to be no obvious positive ground for thinking that *certain shared* psychedelic experiences are not veridical. Moreover, if we shift from theories physical up to theories *metaphysical*, we gain further reasons other than shared experience and noetic feelings to accept certain psychedelic experiences as revelatory, as revealing deeper truths.

For instance, the metaphysician Spinoza argued that mind and matter were but different attributes of the same unified substance: 'God' or 'Nature'. Bertrand Russell wrote that '[o]ne of the most convincing aspects of the mystic illumination is the apparent revelation of the oneness of all things'.[14] If one accepts Spinoza's monistic philosophy, then such a unitive experience under the influence would be very plausibly veridical. In fact, Spinoza himself spoke of a mysterious form of perception he named *amor Dei intellectualis*, 'the intellectual love of God', an experience that was the 'highest possible peace of mind, that is to say ... the highest joy'.[15] God for Spinoza was Nature itself. Thus the unitive and pantheist experiences common to psychedelic states have solid grounds for veridicality in this metaphysics.[16]

Spinoza once met the great inventor of both the calculus and the calculator, G. W. Leibniz. Leibniz was known for his *Monadology*: the view that not only humans, mammals, and the more complex animals have mentality, but also the insects, plants, micro-organisms, etc., all the way down. This is a form of *panpsychism*: that sentience lies within all things that are units, or *monads* (but not aggregates, such as rocks and socks). Panpsychism is a metaphysical view gaining prominence once more today,[17] and again lends itself to substantiating the veridicality of certain psychedelic experiences concerning the sentience and intrinsic value of all the entities of nature.

Thus we see that one's underlying ideology subjectively determines whether or not we understand psychedelic experiences as hallucinations or revelations. The ideology, or faith, of physicalism prevalent today cannot endure as it cannot explain consciousness, let alone psychedelic consciousness. On the other side, believing that *everything* one perceives in the psychedelic state to be veridical is obviously also too much, considering that certain phenomena are *never shared*. It would be implausible to believe in the veridicality of the particular spider that conversed with an artane-inebriated Oliver Sacks 'mostly on rather technical matters of analytic philosophy'.[18] No, the plausibility of the veridicality of psychedelic experiences depends on their having a shared type of experience, one that is coherent with a rational metaphysics, and which can be further fortified by a concurrent noetic feeling. This is what better determines whether a psychedelic experience is considered revelation or hallucination. What, however, complicates the issue further is that 'shared' experiences' may be contingent on culture – for instance, the unitive states experienced in the West often within frameworks from the East are seemingly lacking in the indigenous American psychedelic experience.

Regardless, it may have been such mystical experiences in the West that sired the preference for certain metaphysical frameworks of understanding, above physical ones alone. One seeks to rationalize what one experiences. As Bertrand Russell, who wrote a book on Leibniz, put it in his essay, 'Mysticism and Logic':

> Metaphysics ... has been developed, from the first, by the union and conflict of two very different human impulses, the one urging men towards mysticism, the other urging them towards science.[19]

Notes

1. James, 1902/1982, p. 380.
2. Paz, 1967/1990, p. 88.
3. Donovan, 1979, p. 7.
4. For instance, Zaehner, 1957. For a specific rebuttal of Zaehner's view, see Price, 1963.
5. Non-exhaustively.
6. For example, see McTaggart, 1908.
7. Broad, 1939, p. 164 (my italics).
8. Strawson, 2013, p. 28; repr. Strawson, 2018, p. 154.
9. On emergence, see my chapter 'Panpsychism: Ubiquitous Sentience', in this volume.
10. Kim, 2005, p. 13.
11. See Bradley, 1895; and Popper, 1978. The basic point is that if mentality had no causal powers at all, it would not have evolved in multiple species nor maintained itself. Thus, the evolution of the mental indicates that mental causation must be real. But many physicalists cannot allow for the mental as a fundamental causal power in the universe.
12. See for instance, Kim, 2010, p. 82: '[If sentient objects] were reducible to the causal powers of the base-level [physical] properties, they would have nothing new to contribute to the evolving causal structure of the world.'
13. For a more detailed refutation of physicalism, see Sjöstedt-Hughes, 2019.
14. Russell, 1914, p. 18.
15. Spinoza, B. (1677/2001) *Ethics*, trans. W. H. White and A. H. Stirling (Ware: Wordsworth Classics), V:P32d, p. 248.
16. See Sjöstedt-Hughes, 2022
17. See the first chapter, on 'Panpsychism: Ubiquitous Sentience', in this volume.
18. Sacks, 2012, p. 109. See also the Nietzsche section in the chapter 'The Psychedelic Influence on Philosophy', in this volume.
19. Russell, 1914, p. 780.

V

The Psychedelic Influence on Philosophy

Philosophy itself often arrives as a mind-altering experience, a new mode of perception unto our cosmos, at times so radical as to be hazardous. Thus can philosophy be seen as a psychoactive substance – yet the place of psychoactive substances in philosophy is not apparent. In this cursory and mildly chronological overview we shall shed a little light upon the history of the notable western philosophers who took psychedelic chemicals and how this may have influenced their thought – how psychedelics influenced philosophy.[1]

Plato (c. 427 – 347)

We begin with a radical conjecture: *Western philosophy was partially engendered by the intake of psychedelics*: Plato's philosophy was partly inspired by psychedelic intake, and Western philosophy was partly inspired by Plato. The British philosopher Alfred North Whitehead (1861 – 1947) is known for claiming that, '[t]he safest general characterization of the European philosophical tradition is that it consists of a series of footnotes to Plato'.[2]

Plato is perhaps chiefly known for his arguments for the existence of the *soul* and for the subsistence of an eternal realm of *Forms* ('ideas' that exists beyond space and time). This pair of transcendent notions are encountered first in his book *Phaedo*, also known as *On the Soul*. Their introduction is preceded by these words:

> There are indeed, as those concerned with the mysteries say, many who carry the thyrsus [staff/wand] but the worshipers of Dionysus [the true mystics] are few. These latter are, in my opinion, no other than those who have practiced philosophy in the right way. I have in my life left nothing undone in order to be counted among these as far as possible…[3]

We shall encounter Dionysus, the god of intoxication, later. For now we note Plato's desire to be figured among the philosophers of the Mysteries. The Mysteries were events held regularly in Ancient Greece, the most official and known of which were the *Eleusinian Mysteries* which Plato must have attended – held at Eleusis, a dozen miles or so from Athens. There, at the Temple of Demeter, participants would drink a potion – *kykeon* – containing barley, mint and water. It is widely, though not universally, believed that the kykeon contained too a psychedelic element. What that element was is widely contested, that it was psychedelic is less contested. Dr Albert Hofmann, the creator of LSD, argued that the compound was derived from the barley parasite fungus *ergot*, from which LSD is also derived. Hofmann writes:

> [We can] assume that the barley grown [in the Rarian plain] was host to an ergot containing … the soluble hallucinogenic alkaloids. The famous Rarian plain was adjacent to Eleusis. Indeed this may well have led to the choice of Eleusis for Demeter's temple …[4]

Within the darkened temple, participants had to exclaim: "I have fasted, I have drunk the kykeon". What happened thereafter is, as the name of the event signals, mysterious – but in the *Phaedrus* Plato gives this account:

> [W]ith a blessed company – we following in the train of Zeus, and others in that of some other god – … saw the blessed sight and vision and were initiated into that which is rightly called the most blessed of mysteries, which we celebrated in a state of perfection … being permitted as initiates to the sight of perfect and simple and calm and happy apparitions, which we saw in the pure light, being ourselves pure and not entombed in this which we carry about with us and call the body, in which we are imprisoned like an oyster in its shell.[5]

Thus is it quite plausible that psychedelics inspired the mind-body dualism prevalent in the west, not only in philosophy but also in religion: Plato's influence on Christianity was substantial – Nietzsche even claimed that '*Christianity was Platonism for the "people"*.'[6] Regardless of the validity or not of Plato's arguments, his thinking informed and enlightened our culture. Through a cave darkly, Plato came to see the light; this sunbeam of philosophy, science and reason sprang from the psychedelic experience.

However, dark clouds eventually came to obstruct the sun with the rise of a militaristic Christianity. In 392AD the Eleusinian temples were closed by decree by the Christian Roman emperor Theodosius I. With this the Dark Ages commence, with the light of pagan or secular thought only to return with the Renaissance and then the Enlightenment. The philosopher Immanuel Kant (1724 – 1804) heralds the latter with his anti-Christian essay of 1784, *What is Enlightenment?* Although Kant wrote a book on the scientist and mystic Emanuel Swedenborg (1688 – 1772), Kant himself did not, we assume, have any kind of mystical experiences. However, a follower of his did.

Thomas de Quincey (1785 – 1859)

Thomas de Quincey was one of the first English commentators on Kant, publishing a number of articles on Kant's philosophy of transcendental idealism. Yet what de Quincey is known for above all else is his 1821 book *Confessions of an English Opium Eater*. Therein he describes the psychedelic experiences of the poppy derivative, used at first to sedate his ailments,

> O just and righteous opium! … thou bildest upon the bosom of darkness, out of the fantastic imagery of the brain, cities and temples … beyond the splendours of Babylon … thou hast the keys of Paradise, O just, subtle, and mighty opium!

De Quincey stated his love for three philosophers: Plato, Kant and Schelling. Kant claimed that there existed a reality – *noumena* – beyond our experience, which thus remained inaccessible to us mere humans.[7] Schelling, though a Kantian, argued that perception of noumena was in fact, in a sense, possible[8] – a perception named *intellectual intuition*. Whether de Quincey accepted this Romantic possibility is an open question. Could opium offer a glimpse of noumena or was this but a pipe-dream? Although opium use never made de Quincey go as far as to avow such access to all of reality, it did make him avow the possibility of access to all of one's past. He writes:

> The minutest incidents of childhood, or forgotten scenes of later years, were often revived. … I feel assured that there is no such thing as ultimate forgetting, traces once impressed upon the memory are indestructible…[9]

The indestructibility of memories later became an advanced theoretical issue for the French philosopher Henri Bergson,[10] to whose philosophy the prominent psychonaut Aldous Huxley was in debt, as we shall later see.

Humphry Davy (1778 – 1829)

A contemporary of de Quincey's was the Penzance-born inventor and 'chemical philosopher'[11] Humphry Davy.[12] Davy was friend to the poet Samuel Taylor Coleridge, also an apostle of the Kantian Schelling and his transcendental idealism. Such Idealism – *idea-ism*: that 'matter' in actually is only a projection of the mind – seems to have also come to Davy through high-dose intake of nitrous oxide: 'laughing gas'. In Davy's book on his experiments with the psychoactive substance, he writes:

> I lost all connection with external things; trains of vivid visible images passed through my mind and were connected with words in such a manner as to produce perceptions perfectly novel. I existed in a world of newly connected and newly modified ideas … I exclaimed to Dr Kinglake, "Nothing exists but thoughts!"
> … .
> I have often felt very great pleasure when breathing it alone, in darkness and silence, occupied only by ideal existence.[13]

Though Davy is perhaps viewed as a man preoccupied with concerns of practical utility – he is famed for his invention of the miners' safety lamp, known in fact as the *Davy Lamp* – the apparently non-materialist, idealist experiences bequeathed to him by nitrous oxide seem to have informed his general worldview. In Davy's final book, *Consolations in Travel or The Last Days of a Philosopher*, he writes, against the prevailing materialism of his age and profession, that:

> Without the eye there can be no sensations of vision, and without the brain there could be no recollected visible ideas; but neither the optic nerve nor the brain can be considered as the percipient principle – they are but the instruments of a power which has nothing in common with them. …
> The desire of glory, of honour, of immortal fame, and of constant knowledge, so usual in young persons of well-constituted minds, cannot, I think, be other than symptoms of the infinite and progressive nature of intellect.[14]

Arthur Schopenhauer (1788 – 1860)

Another prominent follower of Kant was the German atheist idealist Arthur Schopenhauer. That title alone shows that an atheist need not be a materialist, despite the common association. Though Schcopenhauer is not known to have consumed nitrous oxide for intellectual pleasure and insight, he did promote the use of other intoxicants for such creative purposes:

> By wine or opium we can intensify and considerably heighten our mental powers, but as soon as the right measure of stimulus is exceeded, the effect will be exactly the opposite.[15]

Whether or not psychedelic substances offer insights from within the experience, at the very least they can offer fuel for intellect and creativity, as Schopenhauer suggests. Schopenhauer did consider the mystical consciousness to begin where the rational philosophical consciousness ends – he saw the former as complementary to knowledge rather than as an obstruction. Furthermore his theory of aesthetics and his reimagining of Plato's theory of Forms could certainly be used to interpret the psychedelic experience. It is a pity that such a great thinker and writer did not pen more on the effects of his drugs. Perhaps this is due to his not taking significant amounts of such chemicals. The figure one could call his successor, however, certainly did take significant amounts of drugs: the antichrist philosopher, Friedrich Nietzsche.

Friedrich Nietzsche (1844 – 1900)

Nietzsche was a professor of philology at the University of Basel from the relatively young age of twenty-four. Under a Schopenhauerian framework, Nietzsche began his philosophical career by writing, in *The Dionysian Worldview*: 'There are two states in which man arrives at the rapturous feeling of existence, namely in dreaming and in intoxication.'

He ends his philosophical career by speaking of his 'inspiration' in terms of hearing thunderous deific voices and stating that he is a *'disciple of the philosopher Dionysus'*[16] – the forest god of intoxication. Between these two statements Nietzsche had ingested a variety of drugs, drugs that may have influenced his culture-shattering philosophy that decried the death of God: *'I am not a man, I am dynamite.'*[17]

Due to chronic migraines, nausea and convulsions, Nietzsche frequently took *opium*. This alone affected his thinking, as can be understood from his letter to close friends:

> My dears, Lou and Rée: … Consider me, the two of you, as a semilunatic with a sore head who has been totally bewildered by long solitude. To this, I think, sensible insight into the state of things I have come after taking a huge dose of opium – in desperation. But instead of losing my reason as a result, I seem at last to have come to reason. …[18]

Nietzsche even devotes two poems in his book *The Joyous Science* to poppy-derived opium. Nietzsche also became a heavy user of *chloral*, ostensibly a sedative. His infamous sister, Elisabeth Förster-Nietzsche, who cared for him regularly, writes: 'In the winter of 1882–3, owing to that terrible influenza, he had for the first time used chloral regularly, in large doses.'[19]

Chloral was taken too in large doses by the late neurologist Oliver Sacks. In his book *Hallucinations*, he describes an experience derived after its intake:

> I went across the road, as I often did, for a cup of coffee and a sandwich. As I was stirring the coffee it suddenly turned green, then purple. I looked up, startled, and saw a huge proboscidean head, like an elephant seal. Panic seized me; I slammed a five-dollar note on the table and ran across the road to a bus on the other side. But all the passengers on the bus seemed to have smooth white heads like giant eggs, with huge glittering eyes like the faceted compound eyes of insects – their eyes seemed to move in sudden jerks, which increased the feeling of their fearfulness and alienness.[20]

Incidentally, with regard to the theme of this article, Oliver Sacks also had a relevant experience on Artane (trihexyphenidyl):

> [A] spider called out "Hello!" ... I said, "Hello yourself," and with this we started a conversation, mostly on rather technical matters of analytic philosophy. Perhaps this direction was suggested by the spider's opening comment: did I think that Bertrand Russell had exploded Frege's paradox?[21]

Bertrand Russell once wrote against Nietzsche that 'I think the ultimate argument against his philosophy, as against any unpleasant but internally self-consistent ethic, lies not in appeal to facts, but in an appeal to the emotions.'[22]

Nietzsche's ethic, or lack thereof, is perhaps encapsulated in the title of his later masterpiece, *Beyond Good and Evil*. In place of the Christian God and His morality, Nietzsche put his ideal of a coming Dionysian age of the Übermensch, the Superman. What the Übermensch actually *is* is an issue of much debate. A. R. Orage who authored the first systematic introduction to Nietzsche in English, writes that:

> [N]ew modes of consciousness will be needed, as the mystics have always declared ... the differencing element of man and Superman will be the possession of these.[23]

And new modes of consciousness did Nietzsche certainly experience. During the August of 1884 when Nietzsche was combining chloral hydrate with potassium bromide, his friend Resa von Schirnhofer planned to visit him in Sils-Maria, Switzerland. After an absence of one and a half days, von Schirnhofer ventures to his house and is led into the dining room – then:

> As I stood waiting by the table, the door to the adjacent room on the right opened, and Nietzsche appeared. With a distraught expression on his pale face, he leaned wearily against the post of the half-opened door and immediately began to speak about the

unbearableness of his ailment. He described to me how, when he closed his eyes, he saw an abundance of fantastic flowers, winding and intertwining, constantly growing and changing forms and colours in exotic luxuriance, sprouting one out of the other. "I never get any rest," he complained…[24]

This is the closest we get to a classic trip report from Nietzsche. Von Schirnhofer also tells us that Nietzsche, as a doctor, was able to obtain any drug he fancied from pharmacists. He was always surprised, von Schirnhofer relates, that they never asked whether he was a medical doctor. A doctor of philology would not have access to the cornucopia into which he immersed himself. Nietzsche's sister and mother claimed that it was this excessive use of drugs, including a later 'Javanese narcotic', which caused his fall into madness and the eventual death that occurred ten years thereafter.

In my book *Noumenautics*, I argued that the rare form of 'inspiration' Nietzsche speaks of in his autobiography is best understood as what would today be labeled *auditory hallucination*, in this case initiated by chemical means. Nietzsche came to hear Dionysus, as Socrates heard his daemon, and eventually he became Dionysus, signing off letters by the god's name. Nietzsche's drugs may have made him into the god that returned to supersede Christ.

William James (1842 – 1910)

Nietzsche was rarely open about his drug use in contradistinction to his American contemporary, the philosopher William James – a deep and often detailed thinker explicit about the potential of psychedelic consciousness for the philosophy of mind and metaphysics. In his book *The Varieties of Religious Experience*, he famously writes:

> Nitrous oxide and ether, especially nitrous oxide … stimulate the mystical consciousness in an extraordinary degree. … [In] the nitrous oxide trance we have a genuine metaphysical revelation.

> ... [Our] normal waking consciousness, rational consciousness as we call it, is but one special type of consciousness, whilst all about it, parted from it by the filmiest of screens, there lie potential forms of consciousness entirely different.[25]

It seems that such chemically-induced insights, catalyzed by the writings of little-known nitrous philosopher Benjamin Paul Blood (1832 – 1919),[26] may have led him to an acceptance of the other forms of consciousness related to the panpsychism and pantheism of Gustav Fechner (1801 – 1887). This metaphysical position James pushed, with the aid of Hegel and Bergson, in his later book, *A Pluralistic Universe* (1909). For instance, James writes,

> The drift of all evidence we have seems to me to sweep us very strongly towards the belief in some form of superhuman life with which we may, unknown to ourselves, be co-conscious. ... The analogies with ordinary psychology and the facts of pathology, with those of psychical research, so called, and with those of religious experience, establish, when taken together, a decidedly formidable probability in favor of a general view of the world almost identical with Fechner's.[27]

Psychedelics did not only help inspire a metaphysical cosmology for James, they also allowed him to claim comprehension of the cosmology of the German dialectical idealist, Hegel (1770 – 1831). In an extensive endnote to his 1882 paper, 'On Some Hegelisms', James writes:

> Nitrous oxide gas-intoxication ... made me understand better than ever before both the strength and the weakness of Hegel's philosophy. I strongly urge others to repeat the experiment ... its first result was to make peal through me with unutterable power the conviction that Hegelism was true after all.[28]

Henri Bergson (1859 – 1941)

On 31st March 1910 Henri Bergson wrote the following to William James:

> ... I believed myself to be to be present before a superb spectacle – generally the sight of a landscape of intense colours, through which I was travelling at high speed and which gave me such a profound impression of reality that I could not believe, during the first moments of waking up, that it was a simple dream. ... How I would like you to pursue this study of 'the noetic value of abnormal mental states'! Your article [*A Suggestion about Mysticism*], combined with what you have said in *The Varieties of Religious Experience*, opens up great perspectives for us in this direction.[29]

Though Bergson himself did not pursue what he thought to be this most valuable path available to philosophy, Bergson is woven into the fabric of psychedelic philosophy due to the fact that his metaphysics was explicitly employed by Aldous Huxley (1894 – 1963), via British philosopher C. D. Broad (1887 – 1971), in what is probably the most famous book on the psychedelic experience, *The Doors of Perception*:

> Reflecting on my experience, I find myself agreeing with the eminent Cambridge philosopher, Dr C. D. Broad, "that we should do well to consider ... the type of theory which Bergson put forward ... The suggestion is that the function of the brain and nervous system and sense organs is in the main eliminative and not productive."[30]

This Bergsonian so-called 'reducing-valve' theory has been very influential in psychedelic circles as a psychophysical account of the psychedelic state. It is the view that the brain, contrary to popular opinion, does not *produce* consciousness but *filters* it according to practical purposes. I have elsewhere offered a detailed explanation of how Bergson's theory can be used to explain the varieties of psychedelic experience.[31] His theory was referred to in connection with the recent brain-imaging studies carried out upon subjects on LSD at Imperial College. This ground-breaking research was sponsored by *The Beckley Foundation*, headed by Amanda Feilding. The findings were launched at The Royal Society in April 2016, where Lady Feilding reflected upon the matter thus:

> Our studies have begun to lay bare the workings underlying the changing states of consciousness. With a better understanding of the mechanisms underlying these states we can learn to use them better, to manipulate our consciousness, to our own and societies' advantage. William James explains it like seeing through the veils of perception. Huxley describes the ego as a reducing valve of the brain. How right they were. Now, for the first time we have seen the empirical basis of these realizations.[32]

The leading scientist (a neuropsychopharmacologist) of this research, Professor David Nutt, made the same point for earlier research on *psilocybin*, a psychoactive chemical within magic mushrooms, in these terms:

> Psychedelics are thought of as 'mind-expanding' drugs so it has commonly been assumed that they work by increasing brain activity, but surprisingly, we found that psilocybin actually caused activity to decrease in areas that have the densest connections with other areas. These hubs constrain our experience of the world and keep it orderly. We now know that deactivating these regions leads to a state in which the world is experienced as strange.[33]

Though this research looks promising for Bergsonians, one should urge caution due to the fact that the neuroimaging research is young and scarce, and our notions of how mind and matter, so named, are related remains a burning question to which no-one has provided a satisfactory answer. Such an answer though, philosophers of mind should note, may require such research – Professor Nutt claimed too that:

> If you want to understand consciousness, you've got to study psychedelics.[34]

Walter Benjamin (1892 – 1940)

Walter Benjamin was enticed into experimentation with hashish and other psychoactive chemicals through his reading of the poet Baudelaire's *Artificial Paradises* of 1860, a book itself inspired by the work of Thomas de Quincey. Benjamin's book *On Hashish* is a posthumous collection of his writings not only on hashish, but also on opium, eucadol and mescaline.

These psychoactive experiments were pursued with his friend, the neo-Marxist philosopher Ernst Bloch (1885 – 1977), who in his chief work *The Principle of Hope* commends the drug's ability to enhance imagination, so vital for human progress.

Benjamin's writings on the psychedelic experience are not systematic, though they contain many sublime fragments:

> You become so sensitive: fearing a shadow would damage the paper on which it is falling ... .
>
> The claims of space and time of the hashish eater now come to bear; and they are regal ... eternity does not last too long.[35]

Sebastian Marincolo argues that apart from the intrinsic value such experiences had for Benjamin, they also had instrumental value in informing the work that made Benjamin noteworthy, especially with regard to Benjamin's notions of *functional displacement* and more specifically *aura*: the spatiotemporal, cultural environment of an object which bestows upon that object a function. One of Benjamin's trip reports reads:

> [T]here is functional displacement. ... [S]omeone gave me one of Kafka's books: "Betrachtung." I read the title. But then the book at once changed into the book-in-the-writer's-hand, which it becomes for the (perhaps somewhat academic) sculptor who confronts the task of sculpting that particular writer. It immediately became integrated into the sculptural form of my own body ...[36]

Marincolo goes on to relate how this noted change of function (from an object to read to a part-role of a body shape) influenced Benjamin's *magnum opus*, *The Work of Art in the Age of Mechanical Reproduction*:

> One of the core ideas of Benjamin's ground breaking essay is to observe that modern means of technical reproduction strip pieces of art of their aura. A photograph of an object can be reproduced and seen anywhere in the world, taking the object out of its spatio-temporal and historical-cultural context.[37]

Benjamin's own historical-cultural context was ill-fated to him, being German Jewish under the Third Reich. Though Nietzsche railed at anti-Semitism, his sister Elisabeth Förster-Nietzsche encouraged it, marrying a leading anti-Semite and befriending Hitler. Such prejudice seems to have ired Benjamin to such an extent so as to have bled into one of Benjamin's mescaline experiences of 1934:

> From the cracks of the Förster House grow tufts of hair. The Förster House: (she [Elisabeth Förster-Nietzsche] has turned the Nietzsche Archive into a Förster House [forester's lodge]) the Förster house is of red stone. I am a spindle in its banister: an obdurate, hardened post. But that is no longer the totem pole – only a wretched copy. Chamois' foot or horse's hoof of the devil: a vagina symbol.[38]

Whilst attempting to flee from the National Socialist regime in 1940, Walter Benjamin died, quite possibly from suicide by morphine overdose. Meanwhile in France another philosopher, for whom Benjamin had only wrath, was lounging and socializing in Paris as an intellectual German army captain: Ernst Jünger.

Ernst Jünger (1895 – 1998)

Jünger emerged into the public eye when he published the recollections of his service as a soldier in the First World War,[39] recollections often considered as glorifications of violence. He was highly decorated for his bravery and aptitude, and later served in the Second World War, as mentioned. However, Jünger twice refused a seat on the Nazi *Reichstag*, and he was loosely associated with Stauffenberg bomb plot to assassinate Hitler – an autocrat whom Jünger perhaps considered a little too left wing.

The philosopher Heidegger, who did join the National Socialist movement, called Jünger 'the true continuer of Nietzsche'[40] – certainly he continued the drug use Nietzsche had pursued. In 1970 Jünger published *Annäherungen: Drogen und Rausch* (*Approaches: Drugs and Intoxication*) wherein he coined the term *psychonaut*: the psychedelic astronaut, explorer of the inner cosmos. This work has still not been published in English, though a Swedish translation exists.[41]

Albert Hofmann was a friend of Jünger and devoted an entire chapter in his book *LSD: My Problem Child* to the man. As with Heidegger, Jünger was in correspondence with Hofmann. One of the letters to the chemist speaks of an aspect of value of the psychedelic experience:

> What interested me above all was the relationship of these [psychedelic] substances to productivity. It has been my experience, however, that creative achievement requires an alert consciousness, and that it diminishes under the spell of drugs. On the other hand, conceptualization is important, and one gains insights under the influence of drugs that indeed are not possible otherwise.[42]

In another letter to Hofmann over a decade later Jünger writes:

> These things should only be tried in small circles. I cannot agree with the thoughts of Huxley that possibilities for transcendence could here be given to the masses. Indeed, this does not involve comforting fictions, but rather realities, if we take the matter earnestly.[43]

Hofmann and Jünger took LSD and psilocybin together on a number of occasions. It seems that the experience had a more profound veridical aspect for Jünger, touching upon matters spiritual, metaphysical, eschatological. Hofmann relates such an occasion:

> The next and last thrust into the inner universe together with Ernst Jünger, this time again using LSD, led us very far from everyday consciousness. We came close to the ultimate door. Of course this door, according to Ernst Jünger, will in fact only open for us in the great transition from life into the hereafter.[44]

Octavio Paz (1914 – 1998)

It is interesting to note that the psychedelic experience does not of necessity lead to a left wing, liberal, or New Age worldview. Jünger is falsification of such a theory. Another follower of Nietzsche and fellow psychonaut, Nobel laureate Octavio Paz, also distanced himself from such a worldview; his psychedelic use fostered a more nihilistic cosmology:

> The Western attitude is unwholesome. It is moral. Morality, the great isolator, the great separator, divides man in half. To return to the unity of the vision is to reconcile body, soul, and the world. ... [Psychedelic] [d]rugs are nihilistic: they undermine all values and radically overturn all our ideas about good and evil, what is just and what is unjust, what is permitted and what is forbidden.[45]

Herbert Marcuse (1898 – 1979)

This view that psychedelic experience can overturn our values is shared by Frankfurt School theorist, Herbert Marcuse. However, returning to the Left, Marcuse argues, in *An Essay on Liberation* (1969), that such an overturn is important not because it leads to a rejection of morality but because it leads to a rejection of capitalism:

> [An] established society imposes upon all its members the same medium of perception ... .

> The "trip" involves the dissolution of the ego shaped by the established society – an artificial and short-lived dissolution. But the artificial and "private" liberation anticipates, in a distorted manner, an exigency of the social liberation: the revolution must be at the same time a revolution in perception which will accompany the material and intellectual reconstruction of society, creating the new aesthetic environment.
> Awareness of the need for such a revolution in perception, for a new sensorium, is perhaps the kernel of truth in the psychedelic search.[46]

Marcuse goes on to argue that such a reset of perception via psychedelics is vitiated if its deliverance of 'artificial paradises' quells the impulse and rationality required to bring about the revolution against the capitalist framework.

Jean-Paul Sartre (1905 – 1980)

The existentialist Frenchman Jean-Paul Sartre was inspired to pursue philosophy due to his reading Bergson.[47] Sartre decided to take an injection of mescaline in 1935 to better understand consciousness, and in hope of generally gaining inspiration. The experience informed his essay *Imagination: A Psychological Critique* (1936) and led to the novel that made him famous, *Nausea* (1938), which features psychedelic imagery. However, for Sartre, the mescaline experience had its price, a price of terror:

> Since I had been experimenting with Lagache, who's rather saturnine and who said to me, "What it does to you is terrible!", I ended up having all sorts of unpleasant images. My first contact with mescaline took place in a partially-lighted room in which all objects changed shape according to real perspective. ... [T]here was an umbrella hanging on a coat rack, and I had the impression it was a vulture. The cloth part of the umbrella became the wings, and then there was a neck and a kind of beak. It was seen like that. ... And when I left I had strange visions,

too. I saw a man as a toad running in the street. And finally, when I got back to Rouen, I saw Beaver's shoe as a big fat fly. ... I immediately foresaw that all this was leading me – why I can't imagine – to chronic hallucinatory psychosis.[48]

This paranoia followed Sartre for weeks after his mescaline experience, as related by the Swedish psychonaut Patrick Lundborg (1967 – 2014):

> For several weeks [after taking mescaline] he had lived with the idea that he was being pursued by giant lobsters. In less fear-stricken moments Sartre understood that the oversized lobsters were not real, but this insight brought him no comfort, since it seemed to suggest that he was going insane.[49]

Michel Foucault (1926 – 1984)

Another French free thinker, who applied himself to Nietzsche's views on power, was Michel Foucault. He took inspiration from psychedelics, taking LSD in a Californian desert in 1975,[50] but he seldom wrote about them. One exception is his essay of 1970, *Theatrum Philosophicum*, which already mentions LSD and opium in relation to Deleuze's Alice in Wonderland book, *The Logic of Sense*. Foucault writes:

> We can easily see how LSD inverts the relationships of ill humor, stupidity, and thought: it no sooner eliminates the supremacy of categories than it tears away the ground of its indifference and disintegrates the gloomy dumbshow of stupidity; and it presents this univocal and acategorical mass not only as variegated, mobile, asymmetrical, decentered, spiraloid, and reverberating but causes it to rise, at each instant, as a swarming of phantasm-events.

Two years before he died of AIDS, Foucault expressed interest in writing: 'a study of the culture of drugs or drugs as culture in the West ... it's so closely tied to the artistic life of the West.'[51]

Unfortunately this study never took place. Concurrently his fellows Gilles Deleuze (1925 – 1995) and Félix Guattari (1930 – 1992), though engaging with talk of psychedelics, frequently with reference to the mescaline use of poet Henri Michaux (1899 – 1984),[52] speak somewhat disparagingly of the value of the drugs, for instance in their book *A Thousand Plateaus*. Such pessimism was in sharp contrast to the optimistic mescaline project envisioned by the psychiatrist who coined the term *psychedelic*: Humphrey Osmond (1917 – 2004).[53]

Outsight

Outsight was the greatest thing that never happened in psychedelia. The project was planned in the 1950s by Humphrey Osmond, neurophilosopher John Smythies, and author Aldous Huxley. The objective was to collect, as Osmond briefed, 'personal reflections on the experience of taking mescaline by 50 to 100 notable subjects in philosophy, literature and science.'[54] These leading intellectuals included C. D. Broad, A. J. Ayer, H. H. Price, J. C. Ducasse, Gilbert Ryle, Carl Jung, Albert Einstein, and novelist Graham Greene. A lot of interest was shown by these figures but, alas, the funding for Outsight was never awarded – a rejection the organizers blamed partly on the stuffy reductivism of the time. It was certainly unfortunate that the first wave of psychedelia occurred concomitantly with the point where the philosophy of mind was at its most reductive. That is, at the point in the West where the intelligentsia favoured, spurned on by arguments in linguistic philosophy and in psychology, a view which reduced the mind to mere verbal confusion, function, physical behaviour or physical identity. Were an *Outsight* re-proposed today, with our less-reductive and multifarious theories as to the mind-matter relation – the 'world-knot' as Schopenhauer called it – funding may be more forthcoming.

Eschaton

Psychedelic experience has then influenced different philosophers in different ways. Its multifaceted, anomalous, alien, awe-inspiring, and at times terrifying nature is not easily analysed. In fact, it often transgresses the phenomenological criteria by which analysis can take place. But then such novel phenomena can be taken as an augmentation of the phenomenological toolkit rather than as a mere mysterious anomaly to treat with philosophic disregard. As A. N. Whitehead urged:

> [The] essence of great experience is penetration into the unknown, the unexperienced … . If you like to phrase it so, philosophy is mystical. For mysticism is direct insight into depths as yet unspoken. But the purpose of philosophy is to rationalize mysticism: not by explaining it away, but by the introduction of novel verbal characterizations, rationally coördinated.[55]

Notes

1. Figures unfairly omitted from this overview include Democritus, Havelock Ellis, Gerald Heard, H. H. Price, W. T. Stace, and John R. Smythies, amongst others.
2. Whitehead, 1929/1985, Pt. II, Ch. 1, §1.
3. Plato, 2002, 69c–d.
4. Wasson, Hofmann, and Ruck, 1978/2008, p. 42.
5. Plato, 1925, 250b–c.
6. Nietzsche, 1886/2008, Preface.
7. See Kant, 1781/7/1998.
8. Schelling, 1800/1997.
9. De Quincey, 1821/1994, pp. 236–238.
10. See Bergson, 1896/1999.
11. As Davy himself writes in his *Consolations of Travel or The Last Days of a Philosopher,* 'Dialogue the Fifth. The Chemical Philosopher' (Davy, 1830/1889).
12. For a fuller exposition, see the chapter on Sir Humphry Davy as the first scientific psychonaut, in this volume.
13. Davy, 1800, pp. 488-491.
14. Davy, 1830/1889, Dialogue Four.
15. Schopenhauer, 1839/2005, Ch. III.
16. Nietzsche, 1888/1992, Foreword, §2.
17. Nietzsche, 1888/1992, 'Why I am a Destiny', §1.
18. Mid-December, 1882.
19. Förster-Nietzsche, 1915/2007, Ch. XXVII.
20. Sacks, 2012, pp. 115-116.
21. Sacks, 2012, pp. p. 109.
22. Russell, 1946/2007, Ch. 25.
23. Nietzsche, 1870/1997, Ch. IV.
24. Gilman, 1987, p. 164.
25. James, 1902/1985, Ch. XVI.
26. See Blood, 1874.
27. James, 1909/1920, Ch. VIII.

28 James, 1882.

29 In Ansell-Pearson and Mullarkey, 2002.

30 Huxley, 1954/2004, p. 10.

31 In *Noumenautics* (Sjöstedt-Hughes, 2015), Ch. IV: 'Bergson and Psychedelic Consciousness'. This was an essay derived from my talk on the subject at the 2013 Breaking Convention conference in London.

32 An extract of this talk was published by *The Huffington Post*: http://www.huffingtonpost.co.uk/amanda-feilding/lsd-brain-imaging_b_9661286.html (12/04/2016; updated 13/04/2016; accessed 21/7/2016).

33 From: www3.imperial.ac.uk/newsandeventspggrp/imperialcollege/newssummary/news_24-1-2012-10-39-58 (24/01/2012; accessed 21/7/2016)

34 https://youtu.be/Sw-OmHFXHs0

35 Quoted in Marincolo, 2015, p. 129.

36 Benjamin, 1927-34/2006, Ch. II (written 15th January 1928 at 3:30pm).

37 Marincolo, 2015, p. 138.

38 Benjamin, 1927-34/2006, Ch. XI (22nd May 1934).

39 In Jünger, 1920/2004.

40 *Gesamtausgabe* IV. Band 90 *Zu Ernst Jünger*.

41 Entitled *Psykonauterna* (see Reference List).

42 Letter dated 3-3-1948 – quoted in Hofmann, 1979, p. 74.

43 Letter dated 17-12-1961.

44 Hofmann, 1979, Ch. 7.

45 Paz, 1959–1967/1983, pp. 83–86.

46 Marcuse, 1969, pp. 36–37.

47 Sartre, 1972/1978, p. 27.

48 Sartre, 1972/1978, pp. 37–38.

49 Lundborg, 2012.

50 See Dean and Zamora, 2021.

51 Interview with Charles Raus – taken from Plant, 1999, p. 152.

52 See Michaux's book (1956/2002) of mescaline experiences, *Miserable Miracle* (which has an introduction from Octavio Paz in its modern form).

53 Osmond first suggested the term in private correspondence to Aldous Huxley in 1956, then published an article using it in 1957.

54 This information was gleaned from Huxley's friend's daughter, in her book *Aldous Huxley's Hands* (Symons, 2015).

55 Whitehead, 1938/1968, Chs. III … IX.

VI

Substance and Process

An Outline

Does some *thing* underlie, or *sub-stand*, change – or is change itself fundamental without need for a substratum? Is there *being* below *becoming*, or is *becoming* below *being*? To adopt the first response is to adopt *substance metaphysics*; to adopt the second is to adopt process metaphysics, or *process philosophy*.

In physics a general shift from substance to process thought was suggested by the realization that electromagnetism did not require an underlying luminiferous aether. Light required no crutches. In biology, there occurred the parallel realization with the theory of evolution: a species had no underlying static, pre-extant design, but rather each species was a transitive phase in a cosmically-long process. In metaphysics, the idea that there was a substance – often as *matter* – underlying all change and thus not itself susceptible to change, was progressively questioned and replaced by thinkers as ostensibly-diverse as Leibniz, Hegel, Peirce, Dewey, James, Nietzsche, and Bergson. This culminated in the systematic process philosophy of Alfred North Whitehead (1861 – 1947), most notably as explicated in his 1929 tome, *Process and Reality*. Process philosophy since then has been predominantly Whiteheadian, and catalysed via the Centre for Process Studies – but there are non-Whiteheadian strands such as those developed by Nicholas Rescher and John Dupré. Though Whitehead is the paradigmatic process philosopher, we glimpse in the fragments of Heraclitus an ancient progenitor: 'All is flux, nothing is stationary.'[1]

Flux, change, becoming, dynamicity, events, process – all antonyms here for purportedly-underlying 'things'. 'Things', in process philosophy, are mere conceptual and perceptual abstractions that mask intrinsic, concrete dynamic processes. The white dot that we sometimes see amongst the stars masks the vast stormy process that we call Jupiter. The white dot that we sometimes see on our plants masks the vastly-complex biological process that we call an aphid. Words, such as 'Jupiter' and 'aphid', seem to gently push the belief in substance metaphysics because words are discrete units seemingly reflecting discrete things. The 'atom' was conceived as the smallest of such things, notably by the Ancient Greek thinker Democritus, his mentor Leucippus, and thereafter Epicurus and Lucretius. Thus can we symbolize the substance-process dichotomy under the opposition Democritus-against-Heraclitus.

Substance

The concept 'substance' has taken a number of meanings throughout the history of philosophy. In western thought these meanings are largely derived from Plato and Aristotle. Pierfrancesco Basile, following Peter Forrest, has a useful list of these various meanings of substance, where the first two meanings ultimately derive from Plato, and the rest from Aristotle:

1. That which truly *is*.
2. That which is capable of action.
3. That which is always a subject of predication and never a predicate.
4. The underlying bearer of properties.
5. That which remains identical throughout change.
6. That which requires nothing else in order to exist.
7. That which is simple (that is, no substance has parts that are themselves substances).
8. That which is not affected from without.[2]

This variety of definitions is ultimately not of necessity incongruous; it can be seen as a range of aspects of the same fundamental notion that substance is that which lies at the base of everything, that to which everything is ultimately *reducible*. In modern thought, we can note a few philosophies that are differentiated primarily upon their use of substance. Material monism (materialism) posits one type of substance: 'matter'. Cartesian dualism posits two: matter and soul (and really, for Descartes a third, God). Spinozism posits one substance: Nature/God (synonyms, for Spinoza). Leibniz posits an infinity of substances which he calls 'monads', each of which perceptually reflect the universe in their own style.

It is, however, materialism (as material atomism) that process philosophy considers the paradigm of substance thinking. As the contemporary process philosopher Nicholas Rescher writes, 'atomism ... is the quintessence of everything to which process philosophy is opposed'.[3] Again, we see the contrast, Democritus-against-Heraclitus. Though ancient, substance thought was solidified further when Galileo re-emphasized the purported division of reality into primary and secondary qualities – where the former was 'matter' in terms of solidity, weight, extension, and so on; the latter, mental qualities such as colour, sound, and emotion. Descartes made the secondary qualities a substance (soul); John Locke accepted the division, and the subsequent dualism, yet maintained that we humans did not really know what upheld, or lay behind, these two substances:

> The idea then we have, to which we give the general name 'substance', being nothing but the supposed, but unknown, support of those qualities we find existing, which we imagine cannot subsist *sine re substante*, without something to support them, we call that support *substantia*; which, according to the true import of the word, is, in plain English, standing under or upholding.[4]

Kant finally argued that we could *never* know that which lay behind the qualities we perceived. Despite Kant's influence, and Locke's caution, it was the substance metaphysics of materialism that held sway as a default position through the Industrial Revolution, as fuelled by such thinkers as Hobbes, Gassendi, de la Mettrie, and Baron d'Holbach. This metaphysics was adopted as foundation of what we today call 'science'. Thus process philosophy, though not anti-scientific, is meta-scientific in the sense that its replacement of science's foundation with process offers a supposedly greater, more parsimonious, overview of reality, with greater opportunities for knowledge. One example of such augmentation is Whitehead's influence upon the formation of the science of epigenetics via C. H. Waddington.

Arguably, substance metaphysics is more conducive to the human mode of cognition. Substance thought has been bolstered by language and a cognitive bias towards spatialization. We shall break up and analyse these in turn, before we approach process philosophy in more depth. We can differentiate two interwoven ways in which language conduces to substance thinking: Through i. Subject-predicate syntax, ii. The noun-verb dichotomy.

i. Subject-predicate syntax

In a proposition such as 'the sun is bright', 'the sun', the subject, is rendered separate from the predicate, 'is bright'. This in turn leads one naturally to consider the subject to refer to a *substance* that is as such something distinct from the *attributes* referred to by the predicate. So the syntax seeds the idea that *something*, such as the sun, *possesses attributes*, such as brightness. Thus the idea is pushed, albeit unwittingly, that underlying changes in brightness, temperature, and suchlike, there exists an underlying, unchanging 'thing'. This bifurcation of substance from attribute is reflected and fortified through predicate logic ('every x is y', etc.) which grounds much of modern thought and technology. The bifurcation grounds much religion in the sense of maintaining a mind-body dualism: the proposition, 'I think' ostensibly separates a soul from its actions. Moreover, retaining the same subject through propositions of morphing tense intimates underlying substance through time. Yet, though useful and perhaps necessary as a condition for communication, syntax and morphology alone are insufficient to demonstrate that reality itself exists in such a divided state. Process philosophy argues that the so-called substance and attribute are one and the same process, falsely divided through such linguistic parsing. The 'brightness' of the 'sun' is *a part, or aspect, of the sun*, it is not an attribute thereof; and the thinking makes the thinker. Both *essential* and *accidental attributes*, so-called, are parts of a process. Moreover, for some process thinkers, the process that is the sun, its radiance, is part and parcel of the process that also involves its being perceived and other so-called 'effects' on its environment. Thus even so-called *relational properties* are not separate from the subject, as subject and object – in addition to substance and attribute – are also one process, divided linguistically yet not actually. Even the words 'cause' and 'effect' falsely divide what is in actuality a unified process.

ii. The noun-verb distinction

As every schoolboy knows, a noun refers to a thing whereas a verb refers to an action – just as above it seems that an adjective (and an adverb) refer to attributes of a thing. Certain languages, such as English, lay greater emphasis on nouns over verbs, thereby subconsciously promoting a substance metaphysics. Alan Watts argues that the Amerindian Nootka language with its lack of nouns and adjectives in favour of verbs and adverbs would more precisely represent the fluctuating actuality of the world.[5] When we analyse the 'thing' that a noun refers to, we find that a verb would be more appropriate. For process thought, a 'thing' is a process that has endured a certain form over time. Whitehead gives the example of the Egyptian stone obelisk Cleopatra's Needle in London.[6] Though it appears to be a long-enduring, unchanging *thing*, it is in fact a heaving flurry of molecular, gravitational, electromagnetic activity that will one day pass away in its current form as an obelisk. In this extended overview, there is no difference in kind between an obelisk and a carnival, between a thing and an event. It is all event. *To be* is a verb.

Spatialization

Our human visual system has in part evolved to outline spatial areas in our environment, distinguished by colour variations. This visualization has the tendency to push the belief that a 'thing' exists as such according to that spatial figure our vision cuts out of reality. In other words, our evolved visual faculty pushes the cognitive faculty into believing that reality is composed of extensive, spatial segments: ultimately leading to atomism. Henri Bergson argues that in truth, '[t]he distinct outlines which we see in an object, and which give it its individuality, are only the design of a certain kind of *influence* that we might exert on a certain point of space: it is the plan of our eventual actions'.[7] That is to say that there is practical, evolutionary advantage in seeing the world as composed of individual bits – but we must be careful to realise how we are being tricked by our biology. In truth, individuality extends beyond that which we see, in space and in time. The sun is more than a sphere at a certain instant. In fact, considering the interfusion of all processes that make up nature, Bergson states that 'individuality admits of any number of degrees, and that it is not fully realized anywhere, even in man.'[8] Furthermore, Bergson argues that even our scientific understanding of *time* has been subjected to our spatial cognitive bias. Real time exists not as a spatial line, a timeline, but rather as the intuited duration that comprises our experience. To cut from such experience, which is always the accumulation of the past into the present via memory, more *bits* – i.e. 'instants' – is as artificial as cutting up the external world into *bits:* atomic particles, etc. The world is not bitty, digital, but instead analogue. 'Substance' is not atoms and instants—such belief is a practical ploy; process is real.

Process

What is a process? The various aspects that address this question comprise the core elements of process philosophy.

1. Substance

This is added not to confuse but to efface confusion. If substance is that which is fundamental, and if there is nothing more fundamental than change, event, or process itself, then one could say that *process is substance*. Even Whitehead writes that, 'If we are to look for substance anywhere, I should find it in events which are in some sense the ultimate substance of nature.'[9] We should also note in this regard that when a profound thinker such as Leibniz uses the word 'substance', it does not thereby exclude him from a processual interpretation of substance.

2. Concrescence and Transition

These are terms Whitehead coins to describe two types of change. Concrescence is internal change; transition is external change.[10] 'Something', as it were, can change in itself – e.g. as growth. Concrescence concerns a single 'actual entity' (a fundamental process of reality), whereas transition concerns the change from one to more such actual entities. Concrescence is ultimately moved by *final cause* (as 'subjective aim') whereas transition is the vehicle of *efficient cause*. Thus, in Whitehead's process philosophy we see the reintroduction of teleology into nature. He writes, 'A satisfactory cosmology must explain the interweaving of efficient and of final causation.'[11] Particles cannot explain purposes.

3. Organic Systematization

Whitehead calls his process philosophy the 'philosophy of organism' because he sees all processes as essentially of the same organic type as those exhibited by organisms. Both a mole and a molecule are organisms, existing as systems (what he calls 'societies') that maintain a form throughout a duration through systematic procedures. There is thus no organic/inorganic dichotomy. These self-systematic procedures transcend the limited notion of autopoiesis to include all entities, all of which have primal experiential elements that cannot be abstracted from their physiology, etc. In other words, organism is the paradigmatic process.

4. Real Time

As opposed to the spatial timeline and the 'instants' so frequently employed by substance metaphysics, as aforementioned in relation to Bergson, process philosophers do not consider time to be an illusion but to be central to actuality. In contradistinction to physicists such as Einstein and certain idealists such as McTaggart who argue for the unreality of time, process philosophers generally accept and accentuate it. As Bergson argues, physics cannot accommodate the speed of time, the direction of time, the specious present: the duration of the present, and it cannot distinguish the past from the present and future – all of which are essential to what time is. Further still, Whitehead adds that at a so-called 'instant', many qualities essential to actualities are lost, for instance velocity, direction, and momentum. An 'instant' is an abstraction, a piece cut out and ripped from reality. It is the elucidation of such cognitive violence that makes for the attraction of process philosophy. To quote Bertrand Russell: 'Dr Whitehead has done more than any other author to show the need of undoing the abstraction of physics.'[12] One tool that Whitehead employs for such undoing is his *Fallacy of Misplaced Concreteness*. Concepts (and percepts) by their very nature pick out certain qualities and always exclude others, so we must urge caution when considering a concept to sufficiently map concrete actuality. Temporal instants and spatial particles are both such abstractions. Whitehead writes that 'Undoubtedly molecules and electrons are abstractions ... . [But] to be an abstraction does not mean that an entity is nothing. It merely means that its existence is only one factor of a more concrete element of nature ... . [The] molecule is really in the event in the same sense as the grin is really on the cat's face.'[13] We may add that, like the Cheshire Cat's floating grin, instants, timelines, and any notions of the reversibility of time, all belong in Wonderland.

5. Contextualism

If a finite, delimited 'thing' is an abstraction, then the concrete reality is a process that flows spatially and temporally beyond its hub and as such interweaves with all other processes. Essential to a process is other processes, none stand in isolation. An 'atom' is an abstraction that in its concreteness includes the environmental forces acting and reacting upon it. It changes with and is dependent upon its environment. This atomic process is everything; there is no unchanging, substantial atom lying beneath this process (this is the abstraction). Thus, in a different scenario an 'atom' is a different entity, a different process. Whitehead extends this wisdom from atoms to genes: 'geneticists conceive genes as the determinants of heredity. The analogy of the old concept of matter [abstract isolated particles] sometimes leads them to ignore the influence of the particular animal body in which they are functioning.'[14] Epigenetics ensued.

6. Realism

Though each subject of experience has their own way of perceiving the world, process philosophy, at least in Whitehead's pivotal manner, is not idealism. The processes perceived by processes such as ourselves exist mind-independently. From Bergson and Whitehead, the relation of sensor to the sensed is no longer one of subject-to-representation but one of part-to-whole. What we sense, we sensors, becomes part of the process that we are. Again, there is no concrete subject-predicate distinction between 'I' and my perceptions, and my identity is not limited to the abstract spatial outline of my body. I am in part that which I see, and what I see is in part, part of me. The intersecting Venn diagram better represents the subject-object relation than does some causal arrow between the separated two. But here we further note that *perception itself is causation*: the influx of the object is a process both perceived and causal (the distinction is another product of misplaced concreteness). Thus does Whitehead refute Hume's rejection of the ability to directly perceive causation. Thus we directly perceive the real world: realism.

7. Creativity and Novelty

Believing in the abstractions that are particles, instants, and constants, led substance thinkers into *determinism*: that one could hypothetically determine the future as the status of such entities could be known (e.g. by Laplace's demon). Determinism thus rejects any freedom of action, any real creation of novel phenomena that could not be theoretically determined in advance. But, when we see through the abstractions, such determinism begins to weaken. Furthermore, we see that it is our consciousness that has created these abstractions, and thus it does not behove the created to determine the creator. Further still, 'constants', or 'laws', of nature are also, for many process thinkers, abstractions that in actuality are also subject to fluctuation. The laws of physics are regularities observed over certain durations of time, nothing more. Even these are subject to change. Consequently, the future cannot be determined and thus creativity reigns (even above the gods for Whitehead). For Whitehead, the electromagnetic era in which we exist will pass, even the three-dimensional spatial universe is subject to change. The future is theoretically unpredictable, and the possibilities for experience are infinite.

— — —

Notes

1. As reported by Plato, *Cratylus*, 402a. In: Waterfield, 2000/2009, p. 41.
2. Basile, 2017/8, Ch. 3, p. 31. Basile notes that this list itself is analogous to one found in Peter Forrest's chapter, 'Sprigge's Spinoza', in: Basile and McHenry, 2007, p. 136.
3. Rescher, 1996, Ch. 2, p. 34.
4. Locke, 1690/1964, p. 186.
5. Watts, 1966/2011, Ch. 4, p. 95.
6. Whitehead, 1920/2004, Ch. 8, p. 166ff.
7. Bergson, 1907/1911/1998, Ch. 1, p. 11.
8. Ibid., p. 12.
9. Whitehead, 1920/2004, Ch. 1, p. 19. Note also that in *Process and Reality: An Essay in Cosmology* (1929/1985), Whitehead states that an '"actual entity" [fundamental process] is a *res vera* [real thing] in the Cartesian sense of that term; it is a Cartesian "substance"' (p. xiii).
10. Whitehead, 1929/1985, Ch. X, §1, p. 210.
11. Whitehead, 1929, Ch. 1, p. 22.
12. Russell, 1927/2007, p. 134.
13. Whitehead, 1920/2004, Ch. 8, p. 171.
14. Whitehead, 1938/1958, Ch. 7, p. 189.

VII

The Great God Pan is Not Dead
Alfred North Whitehead and the Psychedelic Mode of Perception

> Wherefore the current of my soul hath broken
> The bounds of sensual life,
> And I am grown a god, a sinewy token
> Of Pan's most ardent strife;
> I am his own; I seem
> The shadow of his dream,
> *As he is spinning thoughts of form and sense*
> *Out of the formless void, stark, cold and dense.*[1]
> – Victor B. Neuburg

Preamble

Through A. N. Whitehead's metaphysics, the *Philosophy of Organism*, it will be argued that psychedelic experience is a vertical, lateral, and temporal integration of sentience:

I. **Vertical** Integration:
   a. **Superordinate**—upward—partial *apotheosis* (**pan**entheist postulate)
   b. **Subordinate**—downward—partial *enmerosis* (**pan**experientialist postulate)
II. **Lateral** Integration—sideward:
   — Enhancement of *Perception in the Mode of Causal Efficacy*
   — Antithesis of Solipsism
III. **Temporal** Integration—backward
   — Mnemonic Enhancement

— — —

I. a. Partial Apotheosis

Apotheosis, elevation to divinity, is preconditioned by the being of that deific entity. Whitehead's god is both immanent and transcendent, in the traditional senses – but Whitehead's god is not the God of the Judeo-Christian tradition. The god's being is not based on faith but, in part, on the logical necessity of *Eternal Objects* which constitute His transcendent nature.

Eternal Objects are Whitehead's variant of Plato's *Forms*, of Russell's *Universals*, and of Santayana's *Essences*. They are every *potential* form of mentality: ideas (numbers, classes, etc.), emotions (fear, joy, etc.), sensations (colours, tastes, etc.), and other human and inhuman forms. One must be careful to distinguish these *potential* forms of mentality from *actual* forms of mentality. The latter exist *in time* as the subjective phases of an organism, for instance as the thoughts we harbour during the day. The former, the Eternal Objects, can exist in time when they so ingress into actuality; but they mostly subsist *out of time – eternally* – in their unprehended totality.

Viewed thus the *objects* of our mentality are *eternal*, though our mentality is temporal. As the reality of such metaphysical objects may seem dubious to many, let us take an example to demonstrate the reasoning. Consider the sensation *whiteness* as an Eternal Object, or as a *Universal* as Whitehead's student, collaborator and friend Bertrand Russell calls such objects. Russell writes:

> In the strict sense, it is not whiteness that is in our mind, but the act of thinking of whiteness. ... [If] whiteness were the thought as opposed to its object, no two different men could think of it, and no one man could think of it twice. ... Thus universals are not thoughts, though when known they are the objects of thoughts. ... [Universals] subsist or have being, where "being" is opposed to "existence" as being timeless [eternal].[2]

More succinctly yet poetically, Whitehead claims the same point:

> The mountain endures. But when after ages it has worn away, it has gone. If a replica arises, it is yet a new mountain. A colour is eternal. It haunts time like a spirit. It comes and it goes. But where it comes, it is the same colour. It neither survives nor does it live.[3]

Thus whiteness, colours, and all other objects of mentality are deemed metaphysical. Let us delve into the physical to examine the point. A man is seeing a patch of white. Where is this whiteness?

(1) We cannot say it is in the physical object as such, say a cloud. Here there exist the molecules constituting the cloud, which themselves are not white (akin to Berkeley's emphasis[4]).

(2) Further we cannot say that whiteness is in the certain reflected electromagnetic wave as:

(a) the wave without a perceiver will not be white,

(b) the same wave can be perceived as different colours (inverted spectrum, synaesthesia), and

(c) the same perceived colour can have different waves (metamerism).

(3) The whiteness is not actually in the anatomy of the percipient nor in its functioning. It is not in the eyes, nerves, brain: within the skull pervades darkness. The brain does not turn white when intuiting whiteness, as it does not turn triangular when intuiting a triangle.

(4) Though the object that is whiteness is *correlated* with activity in the brain, with the electromagnetic light wave, and with the cloud, this correlate is not thereby determined as *identical* to any of these. Whiteness is neither an *emergent property* of the brain, as such a notion commits the *Emergence Category Mistake*,[5] erroneously presupposing *brute emergence* and an analogy between nature's otherwise *physical-to-physical* acts of emergence (e.g. liquidity from molecules) and a purported *physical-to-mental* emergence. *Emergence is the magic with which materialism is spellbound.*

(5) Whiteness is thus not *identical* (1—3) to its various correlates, it is not an *emergent property* (4) of those subvenient correlates, but nor is it simply the *abstracted common feature* of white objects as this would entail that those objects had the whiteness from which one could abstract it as such. As Santayana puts it, 'Having never been parts of any perceived object, it is impossible that given essences should be abstracted from it.'[6]

Thus, the *object* of a thought, feeling, sensation is, as Russell concludes, 'neither in space nor in time, neither material nor mental; yet it is something.'[7] Eternal Objects are real, transcendent, and the condition of shared experiences – thus they are a condition of language, a condition of knowledge, and for Whitehead a condition for the creative advance of the universe. As Russell put it in *Mysticism and Logic*:

> A truer image of the world … is obtained by picturing things as entering into the stream of time from an eternal world outside … . Both in thought and in feeling, even though time be real, to realise the unimportance of time is the gate of wisdom.[8]

The realm in which all Eternal Objects subsist is named by Whitehead the *Primordial Nature of God*. This is the transcendent aspect of Whitehead's deity, an insentient dimension as sentience requires the ingression of the Eternal Objects into physical temporal actuality to be objects of prehension. As physical organisms, the incessant selection of Eternal Objects is conditioned by our physical needs, and thus only a fraction are positively prehended, the rest rejected through *negative prehensions*, to use Whitehead's terminology. It is my contention that these negative prehensions can be eliminated in degree by the impairment of practical physiological functioning via the intake of psychedelic chemicals. Such elimination entails the integration, nay elevation, of one's consciousness into the primordial nature of this god: *apotheosis*. This is a mysticism without mystical groundings. As Russell foresaw:

> We may hope, in a mystic illumination, to *see* the [eternal] ideas as we see objects of sense; and we may imagine that the ideas exist in heaven. These mystical developments are very natural, but the basis of the theory is in logic, and it is as based in logic that we have to consider it.[9]

George Santayana considered the same spectacle, in horror:

> If I aspired to be a disembodied spirit, I ought to envisage all essences equally and at once – a monstrous requirement.[10]

Such upward integration into the primordial nature of the deity verily may not be joyful, it may evoke intense empyreal dread of the kind Rudoph Otto calls the *mysterium tremendum*, aspects of which include '"daemonic dread" (cf. the horror of Pan)',[11] culminating in the literal *awfulness* that is the original sense of the idea of the holy. As certain Eternal Objects have a being which would usually be ingressed in epochs existing beyond our spatio-temporal, electromagnetic epoch (as Whitehead has it), the alienness of such objects could further the sense of a dread-inducing sublime. Such experiences cannot therefore be categorized as recreation but rather as 'the inmost aim and highest achievement of cognition',[12] as Santayana calls entrance into this realm of Essence *ab aeterno*.

— — —

The other aspect of Whitehead's deity is named the *Consequent Nature of God*. This is the immanent and sentient side. God's function is to initially lure entities into self-formation, then to partake in the intense sentient experiences of them, which, as a *panexperientialist*, as we shall see, includes the autopoetic 'inorganic' – the whole of nature. As Whitehead writes:

> God's purpose in the creative advance is the evocation of intensities. The evocation of societies [higher organisms] is purely subsidiary to this absolute end.[13]

Thus, through psychedelic intake we satisfy the god's purpose, in a league beyond the ordinary mode of mankind. Further still, by allowing upward integration into the hitherto unactualised, thus hitherto insentient, realm of Eternal Objects, we actualize and activate as sentient aspects *of* the god *for* the god. Thus through psychedelic ingestion, *we increase the self-consciousness of the god*. There is no greater divine activity we can pursue than journeying through the psychedelic mindscape – the psychonaut is the pilgrim *par excellence*. Contrariwise, prohibition of psychedelics is the most cardinal of sins.

I say 'the god'. Whitehead came purportedly to regret his use of the word 'God' to designate his deity.[14] His metaphysics is in part a *panentheism* – that god is actuality (as the consequent nature of god) and more (the primordial nature of god transcending actuality). This is already far removed from the *theism* of the Judeo-Christian lineage, the Abrahamic god. Furthermore, as we shall examine, Whitehead's metaphysics is also a *panpsychism*, or *panexperientialism* (as his version is now designated[15]): that all autopoetic entities from man to molecule and below have sentience (though not necessarily consciousness). Whitehead even writes that the,

> function of God is analogous to the remorseless working of things in Greek and Buddhist thought ... the ruthlessness of God can be personified as Atè, the goddess of mischief.'[16]

Whitehead further identified his God with *Eros*, the 'Universe as one',[17] and even, when opposing the Semitic god to Plato's, *Satan*.[18] Thus, with its *pan*entheism, *pan*experientialism, divine mischief and intense hedonism, kinship to pagan animism and its Romantic nature worship, we are better to re-designate the god of Whitehead's philosophy of organism, as *Pan*. We thereby *paganize Whitehead* under the symbol of this seducer goat-god, a god whose desire for the evocation of intense experiences is instanced in his boast of coupling with each of Dionysus' intoxicated Maenads.[19] The lure of Pan is better befitted to the philosophy of organism than the canons of Christ; the latter referring to the attempted Christian hijack of Whitehead's metaphysics under the name *process theology*.

Plutarch relates the story of a sailor who, during the reign of Tiberius concurrent to the lifetime of Jesus Christ, receives over the seas an arcane vocal declaration to propagate the news that "The great god Pan is dead."[20] G. K. Chesterton's pronouncement that 'It is said truly in a sense that Pan died because Christ was born'[21] we now invert across a Nietzschean line. The decline in Christian belief and its offspring, modern cosmology, allows for a revival of a truly naturalistic ontology. God is dead; Pan returns.

I. b. Partial Enmerosis

Enmerosis derives from the prefix *–en*: within, and from *méros*: part or component. The term denotes a downward fusion of sentience into the subordinate entities of the human body.

Before examining the possibility of amplified enmerosis through the psychedelic mode of perception, we must examine the condition for its possibility: *panexperientialism*.

Panexperientialism is the notion that every self-organised entity has sentience: man, mole, molecule and more. There are overwhelming reasons to adopt such a view in the literature,[22] a view espoused by such eminent thinkers as Bruno, Spinoza, Leibniz, Schopenhauer,

Fechner, Nietzsche, William James, and later still, scientists such as the Whiteheadian biologist C. H. Waddington, who founded the new science of epigenetics. But let us appeal to reason rather than to these authorities.

The so-named 'Hard Problem of Consciousness'[23] signals the old problem of understanding how mind can emerge from (or be identical to) 'matter'. Regardless of the complexity of neural activation, why this should be correlated to mental activity remains unexplained. This is because it is unexplainable in the paradigm that reduces explanation to insentient matter moving according to known forces of nature – i.e. to materialism. Sufficiently explaining mind by matter is as successful as sufficiently explaining a squid by the correlated ripples in the sea surface above it. Why?

Whitehead's response to this problem is to state that our idea of 'matter' is an abstraction rather than a concrete reality. In reality, what we call 'matter' already includes sentience, feeling. Thus in vain do we attempt to reconstitute mind from an abstraction that omits it, just as it would be vain to attempt to reconstitute the taste of calamari by the totality of colours which we have abstracted from the creature. *An omitted reality cannot be recreated by the abstractions that omitted it.* This is the cause of the Hard Problem of Consciousness, which is not a problem for the panpsychist.

If one concedes that all of nature, in its organized entities, has sentience, then mind emerges *in degrees* of complexity rather than the problematic emergence *in kind* requisite of materialism. The brain is necessary for complex human consciousness, but the cells of which it is composed are also sentient, as are their components. For Whitehead, the final components are named *actual entities*, or *drops of experience*. Of these sentient drops all actual things are constituted.

The objects of these drops of experience are the Eternal Objects of course, but the actualization of these potential eternal forms is the intrinsic sentient aspect of all that we call matter. Each actual entity in made concrescent by prehending other actual entities which become part of it: *the perception becomes part of the perceiver.* As the actual entities evolve into more complex structures, or so-called *societies*, such as a molecule, the prehended actual entities and the Eternal Objects which determined their form combine to create more complex forms of mentality accordingly: emotions may be augmented by visual qualia, for instance. Feeling, or sentience, is the foundation of all perception however. Perception always includes the transferred internalized feelings of the entity perceived. This transfer, viewed objectively, from the outside, is *efficient causality*. So *perception is causality*. The transfer, viewed subjectively, from the inside, includes *final causality*: each actual entity has a *subjective aim* to achieve the *satisfaction* of a *concrescence* by uniting former actual entities so as to create itself. Thus the determinism we observe is the shell of the teleology of nature – a determinism informed by the mistake of considering observed past regularities as universal constants. For Whitehead the prime tenet that prevails in the universe, above Pan, is creativity. The future can never be determined.

In the highly complex type of actuality that is the human, Whitehead attributes two main forms of perception, which are in actuality fused. There is the classic and commonly accepted *Perception in the Mode of Presentational Immediacy* which is essentially the sensation types from the five senses. David Hume said that all our ideas are copies of these impressions. Hume further argued that with these sensations we can never perceive causality in itself, only the constant conjunction of events. Whitehead, in contradistinction, asserts that we humans do perceive causality (as perception *is* causality). As well as this *Perception in the Mode of Presentational Immediacy,* Whitehead argues that we have *Perception in the Mode of Causal Efficacy*. This is the more primitive form of perception, shared by all organisms – which for him meant all entities of nature, as described above – which is a mode broader and more vague than the former mode, but nonetheless extant. An entity does not need 'sense organs' to sense: all action upon something involves an internal perception in at least the primitive mode of causal efficacy. Sense organs befit larger organisms, bequeathing them with greater means for incorporating their environments. An eye grasps light, a leaf also grasps light sans the fine distinctions made possible by the eye, a molecule also grasps light but in a more primitive sentient causal mode, and reacts accordingly as does the plant and animal. Consciousness is an aspect of the more complex organisms, a blind sentience is the lot of the micro-world. Yet this blindness is not the nothingness of non-panpsychists.

We are never fully conscious of the ceaseless activities of our bodies: the healing of our livers, the battles fought by our leukocytes, etc. Yet the imminences of these bodily cells are vaguely felt by the person, contributing to a sense of health, joy, melancholy, or whatnot. The brain, the dominant organ of control, channels sentience for the overall benefit of the organism, thereby detracting from focus on relatively inessential cellular activity. Psychedelic molecules, which trespass through the blood-brain barrier, wreak havoc on the brain and let slip anarchy into this otherwise ordered channel. As well as the upward integration into alien exogenous Eternal Objects, this may also allow downward integration into the endogenous subjectivities of the subordinate entities of one's body: *enmerosis*.

As stated, Whitehead already allows for enmerosis via perception in the mode of causal efficacy. As this perception is mostly suppressed by our higher form of perception (presentational immediacy) via standard brain functioning, the physical psychedelic breakdown of that functioning will allow the emancipation of those causally efficacious perceptions. Of course, the feelings of these subordinate entities will be foreign in their amplification, perhaps explaining in part the ineffability William James stakes as criterion for the mystical state.[24] Naturally the type of psychedelic chemical and the dose will greatly affect the level of cerebral breakdown. A small dose will not let slip the dogs of war.

II. Lateral Integration

In the words of Whitehead:

> For the external observer the aspects of shape and sense-objects are dominant ... . But we must also allow for the possibility that we can detect in ourselves direct aspects of the mentalities of higher organisms. The claim that the cognition of alien mentalities must necessarily be by means of indirect inferences from aspects of shape and of sense-objects is wholly unwarranted by this philosophy of organism. The fundamental principle is that whatever merges into actuality, implants its aspects in every individual event.[25]

The Problem of Other Minds refers to the problem of knowing how other people and creatures have sentience, as we can only perceive their physical behaviour. It is commonly responded to by claiming inference: I know that I look and behave in a certain way, and I know that other humans look and behave similarly, so I *infer* that those others also have similar minds. We can infer it to other creatures of similar ilk to us: chimps, dogs, goats – but what of insects or plants? We cannot infer it here by analogy, but neither can we simply assume those less-resembling organisms are without mind. To stress the point, consider Thomas Nagel's case:

> [If] things emerged from a spaceship which we could not be sure were machines or conscious beings, what we were wondering about [whether they had sentience] would have an answer even if the things were so different from anything we were familiar with that we could never discover it. It would depend on whether there was something it was like to be them, not on whether behavioral similarities warranted our saying so.[26]

To respond by claiming we could know whether an entity had sentience by whether it had a brain would simply be to postpone the question: how do we know that a brain is requisite for sentience? Is this not blatant *anthropomorphism*? Gustav Fechner, the founder of psychophysics, illustrates the point with elegance when arguing for the sentience of plants:

> If I remove or destroy all the strings of a piano, a violin, a lute, then there will be no tone to the instrument ... so obviously the strings are the essential means for producing tones; they are so to say the nerves of these instruments ... . But now when I hear that the flute after all does actually produce tones, in spite of my pretty argument, I cannot see why plants might not be able to produce subjective sensations without having nerves. The animals might be the string instruments of sensation, and the plants the wind instruments.[27]

Though such an analysis of the problem of other minds here leads to further substantiation of the panexperientialism required for downward integration, are we to rest content with such a mere logical, inferential response to the problem? Whitehead states in the quotation above that the cognition of alien mentalities rests not merely on such indirect inference. The belief that this inference is the highest understanding we can acquire rests on the *assumption* that all perception is perception in the mode of presentational immediacy. When we augment that capability with perception in the mode of causal efficacy, our acknowledged understanding expands.

The prehension of another entity does not merely stand in the relation *representation-to-object* but rather in the relation *part-to-whole*. The prehension of another is the inclusion of that other as a constituent part of oneself. *Perception, like ingestion, is assimilation*. You are what you eat and you are what you perceive. As Whitehead writes, 'no individual subject can have independent reality, since it is a prehension of limited aspects of subjects other than itself.'[28]

In our standard physiological functioning the welter of perception in the mode of causal efficacy is symbolized by the presentational mode.

The sun's rays *causally* hit our eyes and the *causal* line continues in our nerves, all perceived; the Eternal Object of yellow and others ingress for the presentational mode, also thus perceived. Hence even the classic understanding of perception involves causal efficacy, so feeling is always imbued into all sense qualia, and as such the common form of human perception is *actually* this mixed form of *Perception in the Mode of Symbolic Reference*. Illusions occur when this mix is mismatched.

Now, if such standard physiological functioning is impaired through the transgression of psychedelic substances, the symbolic mode of reference is wrecked. *Upward integration* can follow, as argued above, especially when one's environment is scarce of common sense data: in dark, quiet settings. *Lateral integration* can follow in contrary bright open settings where common incoming data are abundant. Now, instead of immediately abstracting away an object due to humanly practical exigencies, named *transmutation* – as is the evolved remit of the brain and body – that is, instead of referring to the object symbolically, the mode of causal efficacy is freed from such symbolic bondage. Now the 'object' is prehended more physically than conceptually, that is more of the object, which has a sentient immanence, enters into the constitution of the 'subject', thereby further fusing the subject-object bifurcation.

Psychedelic reports do include such lateral integration, the advanced form of general *vectorisation*, as Whitehead calls the infusion of prehended objects into the subject. Henri Bergson, a further influence on Whitehead, calls such fusion *sympathy*, the aspect of *intuition* to which Bergson contrasts the conceptual *intellect*.[29] Aldous Huxley made use of Bergson in explaining his mescaline experience, and Huxley's report of becoming one with the legs of the table before him is well-known.[30] Table legs are aggregates of subjectivities as they are not self-organising systems. Of perhaps greater interest lies lateral integration of single, more complex subjectivities. Author Paul Devereux offers this experience on LSD:

> I found my awareness slipping inside that of the daffodil. While still being conscious of sitting in a chair, I could also sense my

petals! Then an exquisite sensation cascaded through me, and I knew I was experiencing light falling on those petals. It was virtually orgasmic, the haptic equivalent of an angelic choir ... A mythic atmosphere hung like the most delicate gossamer in the air.[31]

For the Philosophy of Organism, all perception involves the actual integration of the object into the subject, yet this is always limited by the subject's practical considerations, abstract considerations which led to the supposed solipsism of subject from object. But a Whiteheadian analysis renders solipsism obsolete by highlighting its mistaken assumption: that a perception is distinct from the perceived. *In the psychedelic mode of perception, we thus can move so far from solipsism that we enter the subject of the object.*

III. Temporal Integration

Hence, in the psychedelic mode of perception we push our identity with Pan through our integrated panentheism and panexperientialism. We thereby touch the eternal and the present, but what of the past? The past is not actual, potential but neither is it nothing. For Whitehead, all actualities pass into *objective immortality*: they are no longer subjectivities but their physical and mental forms enter into the composition of actual entities and their *nexūs*, forms of togetherness.

All perception involves perception of the past: memory. But again, those aspects commonly selected are those that are conducive to the practicalities of the organism. Furthermore, a memory is immortalized as an Eternal Object in the empyrean realm that is Pan. Thus these objects are never absolutely lost. Analogous to the emancipation from transmutation offered in lateral integration, the psychedelic mode of perception can allow for a backward integration. This is part of the basis for contemporary studies into the value of psychedelic therapy.[32] Thus, psychedelic intake enhances access to distant memories, access to the objective immortality, emphasizing Whitehead's words that:

> What is done in the world is transformed into a reality in heaven, and the reality in heaven passes back into the world.[33]

This heaven is often a hell, which is the bane of the sufferer and the object of the therapist. Pan is not omnibenevolent. So it is not 'morally necessary to assume the existence of God', as Kant argued,[34] but it is logically necessary to assume Eternal Objects which can be named after a less Christian god. Through this god backward integration can occur – also to an extent inversely related to practicality – as one of the first English commentators on Kant, Thomas de Quincey, recounted for an opium-induced experience:

> The minutest incidents of childhood, or forgotten scenes of later years, were often revived ... placed as they were before me, in dreams like intuitions, and clothed in all their evanescent circumstances and accompanying feelings, I recognized them instantaneously. ... I feel assured, that there is no such thing as forgetting[;] traces once impressed upon the memory are indestructible.[35]

We have thus vertical, horizontal and backward integration in the psychedelic experience. The question concerning forward integration remains: actual foresight. In the Philosophy of Organism this is not possible as the future is not determined and thus does not exist in its entirety. Creativity primes the advance of the universe, with its free teleology of entities – thus the future is not yet existent, it is not yet created. Therefore it cannot be foreseen. However, in upward integration, Eternal Objects can be experienced which would otherwise have their common ingression in future epochs – including non-electromagnetic epochs. Thus a slight foresight of potential mentalities can be made manifest, though not a foresight of actual events.

Summary

The psychedelic mode of perception allows for a three-dimensional integration of experience: the vertical dimension *upward* to primordial Pan and *downward* into endogenous primitive pieces of perception, understood through panexperientialism. The lateral dimension is that along which we can integrate *sideward* into the other exogenous entities constituting our environment. The temporal dimension can push us *backward* to memories otherwise lost, and fragmentarily *forward* in terms of glimpses of future types of sentience. These dimensions offer a panopticon of Pan, Nature Himself – experiences of Nature otherwise masked by our practical needs. Psychedelic perception bursts practicality, opening philosophy to greater streams of enquiry.

― ― ―

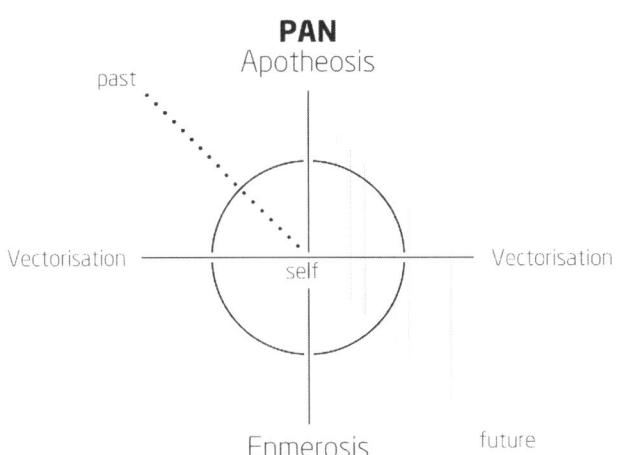

Notes

1. Neuburg, 1910/2009, §VI.
2. Russell, 1912/1980, Ch. 9.
3. Whitehead, 1925/1967, Ch. V, pp. 86–87.
4. Consider George Berkeley's words: 'all the colours we see with our naked eyes are only apparent – like those on the clouds – since they vanish when one looks more closely and accurately, as one can with a microscope.' (1713/2015, First Dialogue.)
5. See Griffin, 1998, Ch. 6, §III, p. 65.
6. Santayana, 1923/1955, Ch. X, p. 94.
7. Russell, 1912/1980, Ch. 9.
8. Russell, 1914, §III.
9. Ibid. I have argued elsewhere that Plato's theories of Forms and of Dualism were quite possibly inspired by such a deific vision induced by psychoactive substances taken in the Eleusinian Mysteries – an inspiration which itself inspired western philosophy. See my public lecture given at the University of Exeter (10th March 2016): youtu.be/X2eY4n37FC0
10. Santayana, 1923/1955, Ch XIV, p. 132.
11. Otto, 1923/1958, Ch. IV, p. 14.
12. Santayana, 1923/1955, Ch XIV, p. 128.
13. Whitehead, 1929/1985, Part V, Ch. III, §X, p. 105.
14. See Griffin, 1998, Ch. 9, §IV, p. 204.
15. 'Panexperientialism' was coined for Whitehead's version of panpsychism by David Ray Griffin in *Mind in Nature: Essays on the Interface of Science and Philosophy* (co-edited with John B. Cobb), 1978.
16. Whitehead, 1929/1985, Part III, Ch. III, §I, p. 244.
17. Whitehead, 1933/1967, 11, p. 295.
18. Whitehead, 1929/1985, Part II, Ch. III, §III, p. 96.
19. See Graves, 1955/2002, Vol. 1, Ch. 2, p. 102.
20. Plutarch. *De Defectu Oraculorum*, §17.
21. Chesterton, 1925, Part I, Ch. VIII.
22. Access www.philosopher.eu/panpsychism for a list of live texts.
23. Coined by David Chalmers, 1995.
24. James, 1902/1985, Ch. XVIII.
25. Whitehead, 1925/1967, Ch. IX.
26. Nagel, 1979/2012, Ch. 13 ('Panpsychism').

27 Fechner, 1848.
28 Whitehead, 1925/1967, Ch. IX.
29 Bergson, 1911/1998, Ch. II, p. 176. William James expands upon this notion in *A Pluralistic Universe* (1909/1996).
30 Huxley, 1954/2004.
31 Devereaux, 1997/2008, p. 27.
32 See, for instance, Carhart-Harris, et al. 2016; or Sessa, 2016.
33 Whitehead, 1929/1985, Pt. V, Ch. II, §VII, p. 351 [532].
34 Kant, 1788/2002, Book 2, §1-2.
35 De Quincey, 1821/1994, pp.236–238.

VIII

The Pentalogy of Perception

In this exposition, the five essential elements of perception are listed and explicated, viz. sensing, perceptons, ecto-physical correlates, endo-physical correlates, and demeteptions. The differentiation that calls for such neologisms is important for wider discussions about the mind-matter problem – when a writer refers to a 'perception' and its relations, the word can denote to readers any of these five elements. By clarifying such distinctions, it is hoped that the mind-matter problem is aided.

Let us briefly enumerate these five elements. By *sensing* is meant the *temporal* action of being sentiently affected by the spatiotemporal environment. By *percepton* is meant the *atemporal* qualitative object or type of a perception (the colour, the scent, etc.). By *ecto-physical correlate* is meant the physicality external to the perceiver that is partly causative of the perception. By *endo-physical correlate* is meant the bodily correlates of sentience. Lastly, by *demeteption* is meant perceptions that are not sensings of the physical environment.

– – –

The word *perception* – etymologically a combining of *per* (by means of) and *kap* (taking, grasping) – is a word used in many different senses depending on discipline and even within a single discipline. This multifarious denotation commonly conduces confusion. I here want to briefly distinguish five aspects, a pentalogy, of perception so to stall such potential misunderstandings. The pentalogy is composed thus:

1. Sensing
2. Percepton
3. Ecto-Physical Correlate
4. Endo-Physical Correlate
5. Demeteption

1. Sensing

Sensing is the *temporal* action of being sentiently affected by the spatiotemporal environment. Perception is more than sensing because we can also be sentiently affected by things other than our environment – e.g. we perceive the objects in our dreams (see point 5 on demeteption below). The senses traditionally, for instance as Plato listed them,[1] are those that are visual, auditory, olfactory, gustatory, and haptic. The last, touch, is better expanded as *somatic sensation* so to include proprioception, temperature, and other bodily feelings. Although the listing makes these senses seem discrete, there are symbiotic overlaps such as the olfactory and gustatory, and gustatory and haptic (one tastes by the touch of one's tongue). In addition to these traditional modes of sensing, the philosopher A. N. Whitehead adds what he calls *perception in the mode of causal efficacy*[2] (PMCE), which is a primitive, vague received feeling of externality. This is the direct causality of the environment into us, which is felt as such. Only through this direct sensing of external reality do we avoid solipsism, overcome Hume's problem of causation,[3] and explain our common feeling of the reality of that which we sense. For humans, the traditional five senses are at the forefront of our perceiving, with PMCE as a generally subconscious mode (thus neglected in the literature) – but in more primitive organisms PMCE is the only form of perceiving – one needs not the traditional 'sense organs' to sense: a plant senses light yet has no eye.

Sensing, and perception generally, need not be conscious by which is meant *access conscious*,[4] i.e. aware. We are generally not conscious of the myriad elements of any of our *percescapes*[5] – for instance, we need not be *conscious* of all the varieties of colour in our present visual field though we *perceive* them.[6] Perception can thus be subconscious – and even when conscious, perception is only a part of consciousness. When perception is subconscious, it is still an aspect of the broader *sentience*: the subconscious is not non-mental. In this sense we must distinguish *subconscious sensing* from *unconscious receiving*: a mechanical camera can receive and record the effects of light, but as it is not sentient – neither subconscious let alone conscious – and so as to avoid confusions and conflations down the line, it is better not to say that a camera, or any other so-called 'sensing' machine, *senses* – rather, it *receives*. A radio does not sense but receives a broadcast. Thus can we distinguish the actions of conscious sensing, subconscious sensing, and receiving.

2. Percepton

A percepton is an atemporal object of a sensing and of a *qualial demetept*[7] – it is the sensual universal. It is important for many discussions, especially concerning the mind-matter problem, to differentiate the temporal *action* of sensing (above) from the *objects* of that sensing

– the act of perceiving from the objects that are: perceptons (2), and ecto-physical correlates (3). My perceiving of a specific colour (2) is not itself that colour, just as my perceiving of a plant (3) is not that plant. The plant exists spatiotemporally external to me, and the colour exists atemporally (eternally) external to me. But surely, someone may protest, the colour simply *is* its being perceived. Were that the case, a person could never see the same colour more than once, and another would never be able to see it. In the words of Bertrand Russell:

> if whiteness were the thought [the perceiving] as opposed to its object, no two different men could think it, and no one man could think it twice. That which many different thoughts of whiteness have in common is their object, and this object is different from all of them.[8]

The whiteness is a *percepton*, the act of seeing it is a *perceiving,* or (more narrowly) a *sensing.* Just as we do not say that the perceiving of a cloud *is* the cloud, so we should not say that the perceiving of whiteness *is* the whiteness. The cloud is an external temporal correlate (3) of its being perceived, and 'its colour' is an external atemporal correlate (2) of its being perceived – though (2) and (3) are contingently related (see below). The percepton is atemporal, eternal, because, it cannot be identical to any temporal manifestation in the mind nor to any temporal manifestation in matter (see [3] and [4] below), yet we cannot deny its reality – just as we cannot deny the reality of the eternal Pythagorean Theorem, regardless of whether it ever were thought or physically applied, as the logician Frege declared.[9] Existence transcends the spatiotemporal.[10] In this sense, perceptons are neither mental nor material, but they can manifest mentally (as objects of perceiving and demeting[11]) and as such as representations of what we call matter.

Thus do we distinguish the act that is sensing (1) from that which is sensed ([2] and [3]).

3. Ecto-physical Correlate

This term refers to the physicality external to the perceiver that is partly causative of the perception. For instance, when I *feel heat* the ecto-physical correlate is the intruding high molecular motion and/or radiation. In both cases we are speaking of forces of energy, and it is energy combined with spatiotemporality that predominantly defines our concept of physicality.[12] It is a common error to say that heat *is* molecular motion, an error that causes further errors.[13] Heat is the occurrence (1) of a felt percepton (2), which occurrence *can in part be caused by* specific ecto-physical correlates (i.e. molecular motion and/or radiation). To say that heat *is* molecular motion is as confused as saying that happiness *is* a cigar. Cigars can partly cause happiness, and molecular motion can partly cause the feeling of heat. Unfortunately this error has been somewhat cemented by language, as we can refer to both the feeling ([1] and [2]) and the ecto-physical correlate (3) by the same word: 'heat'.

Likewise is it with vision. It is error to say that redness *is* electromagnetism of a frequency between 430 and 480 THz. Rather, a specific redness (2) may be the object of a sensing (1) that is in part caused by a specific electromagnetic frequency. If there were no one to see it, the electromagnetic wave would not become the colour; and inversely, we can *imagine* (5) the colour without the need for the electromagnetic wave – thereby revealing the distinction. To reveal further still: different waves can be sensed (1) using the same colour (2), a phenomenon known as *metamerism*.

In addition to this, it is well-known that the visible spectrum is but a fraction of the entire electromagnetic spectrum. Insects can perceive ultraviolet ranges therein to which we are blind. This also makes clear the distinction between the wave and a perceived colour. There is a further twist still: *that certain ecto-physical forces should correlate to certain specific perceptons is arbitrary*. That an electromagnetic frequency of 450 THz should correlate to a *red* percepton is not a logical or empirical necessity (though it is commonly contingently observed). In fact, due to the possibility of *inverted spectra* (which John Locke highlighted)[14] we do not even know that each human has the same percepton for the same ecto-physical correlate. I may see a darker red than you see whilst we together gaze upon the same sunset. In fact, it is logically possible that a specific ecto-physical correlate may be causative of a completely different class of percepton than is common – someone may hear light or see air waves. In the condition of synaesthesia this indeed can occur. Other animals may correlate classes of perceptons to kinds of ecto-physicality completely alien to humans – a bat may use vision for its echo-location (colour for its hearing), or perhaps a class of percepton of which we humans are absolutely unfamiliar. If only we knew what it was like to be a bat. Again we see here the need for the distinguishing of an act of sensing ([1], e.g. echo-locating), the percepton ([2]: the object type of the sensing), and the physical energy (3) that is (with the previous factors, and the next below) partly causative of the perception. We also realize that there can exist a far higher number of perceptons than those to which we humans are prosaically privy: more colours, more sounds, more scents; moreover, perceptons of more *kinds* than we could ever conceive (beyond colours, sounds, etc.); and still yet: experiences of types beyond perceptons, conceptons,[15] and other common human modes of experience. Logically, the quantity of such eternal experiential types is infinite.[16] Perhaps certain humans have more perceptons than others, perhaps some chemicals can aid our expansion thereof. As William James famously concluded after nitrous oxide self-experimentation:

> our normal waking consciousness ... is but one special type of consciousness, whilst all about it, parted from it by the filmiest of screens, there lie potential forms of consciousness entirely different.[17]

4. Endo-Physical Correlate

An endo-physical correlate is the concurrent bodily physical activity subvening the perceiving (or any other act of sentience). Usually in the literature this is limited to the 'neural correlates of consciousness', lying in the brain. But due to factors such as: (i) that these correlates have not been fully empirically determined, (ii) multiple realization,[18] (iii) the plausibility and thus ever-gaining acceptance of panpsychism,[19] and (iv) due to the multiple meanings of 'consciousness',[20] it is safer to use the term, the *physical correlates of sentience*.

Just as it is error to say that a colour *is* its common ecto-physical correlate (i.e. electromagnetic wave), so is it error to say that a colour *is* its endo-physical correlate (e.g. activity in the visual cortex). The colour is what it is (2), regardless of its being seen (1), of its external part-cause (3), and of its physical substrate (4). A perception cannot be *identical* to its endo-physical correlate because of the possibility of multiple realization (see note 18), and for example, because of the so-called 'property objection': (4) has properties which its (2) has not. And thus, by the *principle of the indiscernibility of identicals*,[21] (4) cannot *be* (2). For instance, a neural process has a fluctuating length, breadth and depth, and a certain mass; whereas the object of the sentience of which it is a correlate may not as such have any (let alone the same)[22] length, breadth and depth, nor mass (e.g. navy blue) – thus they cannot be exactly one and the same, despite correlation.[23] Darkness, not navy blue, dwells within the skull.

5. Demeteption

This neologism refers to perceptions that are not sensings of the physical environment. These can be experiences that are, as it were, *cultivated* by us[24] rather than by ecto-physical correlates. I name the type after the goddess of agriculture, *Demeter*. A common mode of demeteption is *imagination*: images that appear before us, not directly caused by external physical objects. But the term *imagine* (for such demeteption) is unsatisfactory firstly because it also connotes falsity – as H. H. Price wrote: 'Paradoxical as it may sound, there is nothing imaginary about a mental image.'[25] Secondly, the term is prejudicial to all but the sense of vision – to say that one can '*imagine* a sound', a non-*image*, can lead to later confusion and, moreover, it hurts the ear and the intellect. One demetes a sound. Although demeting is not sensing (1), as it is not perceiving the immediate ecto-physical, a demetept may be a sensible percepton (e.g. imagining a missing shade of blue). Thus 'demeting' is the insensible temporal act of experiencing an atemporal percepton. The percepton of demeting is named a demetept. Demetepts include more than mere imaginations: they include dreams (lucid or not), episodic memories, hallucinations, hypnagogic hallucinations, psychedelic mindscapes, subconscious phenomena, and other 'mystical states'. In other words, experiences that have no immediate (synchronic)[26] ecto-physical causes. Though a demetept can be a percepton (and thus is included in this pentalogy of perception), a demetept also can be of an emotional variety (one can, as it were, 'demete an emotion'), and of other types of objects of sentience.

The purpose of including demetepts within perception is not only to offer an adequate taxonomy, but to emphasize that a perception cannot be identical to any external physical wavelength, or interaction therewith. Perception need not be extended outwards in this way. It is often said that a perception part-caused by an ecto-physical object is *veridical* (i.e. it truthfully represents reality) whereas a perception that is not so-caused is non-veridical (i.e. not representative of reality). However, if it is accepted that non-physical objective realities (such as mathematical truths and perceptons) are partly-causative of their perception, then the aforementioned criterion of veridicality is inadequate, as a demetept here would be veridical. Kurt Gödel, for instance, posited this.[27] Though of course it must be accepted that a hallucination is a demeting (5) of perceptons (2) that is cognitively misclassified as caused by an actuality (e.g. 3).[28]

– – –

Thus is presented the pentalogy of perception – which itself is only a part of *sentience* (which also involves conception, emotion, expectation, intention, aesthetics, rhythms of duration, reason, levels of awareness, etc.). But when someone speaks of a *perception*, we should refer to the pentalogy so to ask whether that person is referring to: (1) the act of *sensing*; (2) the *percepton* perceived, such as a colour, a sound; (3) the *ecto-physical correlate* which in part (along with certain of these other points) causes the ingression of the percepton into the act of sensing; (4) the *endo-physical correlate* that is known to accompany a percepton, though it cannot *be* that percepton; and/or (5) is that person referring to *demetept*: a memory, a dream, the appearance of an irreverent machine-elf? Such are the basic aspects of perception, distinctions that can prevent one's being piskie-led whilst exploring the mind-matter mystery.

— — —

Notes

1. Plato, c.360BC/1965/1976, pp. 85–94 (61–69).
2. See for instance *Symbolism*, 1927/1985, ch. II, §§1–4.
3. Because we *do*, contra Hume (1739–40/1985, p. 295–6), directly perceive causality. This renders Kant's later transcendental idealism partly redundant.
4. See Block, 1995; and Block and MacDonald, 2008.
5. That is, the fields of perception around us including our visual field, auditory field, etc.
6. We may even demete many of the colours in our percescape (see point 5).
7. See Point 5 for the description of a demetept. A *qualial demetept* is that class of demetepts associated with the human senses (e.g. colour, sound, etc.), as opposed to emotions.
8. Russell, 1912/1980, p. 57.
9. Frege, 1918–19/1956, p. 301.
10. Even a sceptic of such Platonism might at least acknowledge that differentiating the object (2) and its being perceived (1), regardless of the former's ontological status, will aid discussion.
11. See point 5.
12. Though note that the concept of physicality is vague and shifting, and certainly not settled. See, for instance, Feigl, 1967: 'to say "x is physical" is highly ambiguous' (p. 58).
13. For example, by this conflation Kripke is in part led to a flawed critique of psychophysical identity theory (e.g. 1971).
14. Locke, 1690/1964, Ch. XXXII, §15, p. 246
15. A *concepton* is the eternal object of a temporal conceiving.
16. *Eternal* means timeless; *infinite* means without end. Thus there is no tautology in the statement to which this is a note.
17. James, 1902/1985, p. 388.
18. *Multiple realization* is the idea that a mental state, such as hunger, can have multiple endo-physical correlates: such as those of a human and those of an octopus (meaning that the mental state cannot be identical to the endo-physical state). See, e.g. Putnam, 1973.

19 Panpsychism: that minds exist fundamentally and universally. See the first chapter in this book.

20 For instance, 'consciousness' for some relates (understandably) only to *conscious* as opposed to *subconscious* states of mind, with the implication that the term 'neural correlates of consciousness' is inappropriate as it refers really to all states of sentience.

21 If x and y share exactly the same properties, x and y must be numerically identical. $(x)(y)([F][Fx \equiv Fy] \supset [x=y])$. See Rosenbaum, 1977.

22 We must, however, posit *twofold space* for visual and somatic perceptons. See Bradley, 1895; James, 1904; and Russell, 1948/2009, ch. 6, pp. 192–196; and Chapter X in this volume.

23 Though they could both be aspects of the same thing – in the manner of Spinozism for instance. But as aspects, they are distinct.

24 Though note that demetepts are also part-caused by eternal objects, and possibly other non-physical (i.e. non-spatiotemporal) objective realities.

25 Price, 1953, p. 4.

26 I write *synchronic* because a demetept may have a diachronic ecto-physical part-cause (such as is the case for the episodic memory of a physical event).

27 See for instance Wang, 1987, pp. 188–192.

28 I write 'e.g. 3' because a hallucination might *also* be cognitively misclassified as being caused by an actual though non-physical spirit.

The First Scientific Psychonaut
Sir Humphry Davy

Visionary power
Attends the motions of the viewless winds,
Embodied in the mystery of words:
There, darkness makes abode, and all the host
Of shadowy things work endless changes…[1]
– William Wordsworth

'To fathom Hell or soar angelic, just take a pinch of psychedelic'[2] – penned in the mid twentieth century, this was the rhyme that coined the word 'psychedelic' and inaugurated its scene. The scene was soon suppressed, to the extent that no-one would have believed then that in the first decades of the twenty-first century human affairs would occupy themselves once more with mind-altering chemicals. Yet here we find ourselves, within the whirls of the so-named 'psychedelic renaissance'. Author Michael Pollan expresses, and thereby assists, the revival thus:

> Today, after several decades of suppression and neglect, psychedelics are having a renaissance. A new generation of scientists, many of them inspired by their own personal experience of the compounds, are testing their potential … hoping to unravel some of the mysteries of consciousness.[3]

But there are more than several decades of neglect. Over two centuries ago, Penzance's great scientist, 'chemical philosopher' Humphry Davy had pioneered experimentation with mind-altering compounds not merely in a quantitative, clinical fashion, but in ways, upon others and upon himself, philosophical: phenomenological and metaphysical.

We shall see how Davy, to be introduced, experimented with nitrous oxide, in increasingly large and frequent doses, till he attained experiences sublime. As well as being a published poet, Davy also pursued speculative metaphysics, as gleaned from his notebooks, letters, and especially his final, extraordinary book, *Consolations in Travel; or, The Last Days of a Philosopher*. Davy's interest in idealism, catalysed especially through the interests of his friends Coleridge and Wordsworth, and their mutual interest specifically in Spinozism, will be analysed in respect to Davy's phantastic 'visions', 'spectra', trips – experiences of the Absolute, of empyrean spacescapes, of alien beings forging communication. It is no exaggeration to say Davy – with all respect to Paracelsus, Robert Boyle, and Robert Hooke[4] – was the first scientific psychonaut.[5]

Who was Humphry Davy? Born on the 17th December 1778, dead on the 29th May 1829, Davy was a quick burst of human light. In 1800 he publishes a book on the chemical and philosophical properties of nitrous oxide, the 'laughing gas' intake of which becomes a recreational activity soon thereafter in British aristocratic circles, before becoming an attraction in the US, where it is first used as an anaesthetic in 1844 (first produced commercially by the cousin of Edgar Allan Poe). In 1807 Davy discovers potassium, and in following years other elements such as calcium, barium, and magnesium. In 1812 he is knighted, only the second scientist to be thus awarded after Isaac Newton. Three years later Davy invents the famous miners' safety lamp, lovingly described simply as the 'Davy Lamp', a device that saved many lives by preventing explosion, and the one thing that the Davy statue holds, proudly. In fact, it is in relation to this lamp that he is predominantly known, his other subterranean visions of light remaining generally unknown.[6] In 1820 Davy is elected President of the Royal Society, the world's oldest independent scientific academy. Davy dies in Geneva at the age of fifty, having suffered ill health for three years beginning with his first stroke in 1826 – with following pains appeased somewhat by opium.[7] He had finished his book *Consolations* just before he died, and it was published via his brother John the following year in 1830. This book, Davy wrote in a letter, 'contains the essence of my philosophical opinions',[8] which is a rather bold statement from a man of science, considering the book's highly mystical and visionary tone, as will be seen.

Davy was born in the harbour town of Penzance, within the Celtic land of Cornwall, culminating Britain to the south west. Not only does Cornwall bear the romanticized history of pirates and mermaids, tin miners and their hypogean goblin knockers – but Arthurian legends, and shadow talk of druids ritualizing at the stone circles, quoits, and fogous that lie strewn across the raw beauty of ancient-hedge-enclosed moors and meadows. Davy was infused and enthused by such surroundings, to which his early poetry attests. Both his parents were of Cornish stock, his ancestors described as yeomen and gentlemen on their Ludgvan tombstones – his paternal grandmother was reputed to have second sight.[9] Davy was an average schoolboy, but, in his late teens, began a self-imposed self-education.[10] Much of this involved metaphysics, including the study of figures such as Locke, Hartley, Berkeley, Hume, Helvetius, Condorcet, adding to his school study of the ancient Lucretius who, along with the rebellious streak weaving through his notes, may have inspired Davy's early sympathies with materialism (which he came to reject).[11] In later years he wrote, without apology, 'What I am I have made myself'.[12] Davy's quick metamorphosis was even a shock to his close friend Gregory Watt,[13] who, when visited by Davy in Birmingham, was, Mike Jay writes,

> astonished to encounter not the previous winter's wild Cornish lad but a confident and extrovert figure at the hub of a sophisticated philosophical circle.[14]

In his teenage years Davy was apprenticed at Peasgood's Pharmacy which stood atop Penzance's main artery, Market Jew Street – a pharmacy that was later to find itself beside the statue of Sir Humphry Davy, erected in 1872. Back in 1798, at the age of twenty, Davy was invited to work in Bristol, two hundred miles from Penzance, at the newly-formed Pneumatic Institution – a centre created by a Dr Thomas Beddoes chiefly to research and apply gaseous methods to treat illnesses, primarily tuberculosis.

Davy's chief preoccupation there was to see if nitrous oxide, discovered in 1772 by the English theologian, chemist, and liberal radical Joseph Priestley, was, as American physician Dr Samuel Latham Mitchell had claimed in 1795, highly toxic. Davy quickly showed through experiment that this was certainly not the case, in fact, the truth was quite the contrary.

To be sure, on 11th April 1799 Davy inhaled, for the first time, *pure* nitrous oxide, without any untoward effects – as opposed to the carbon monoxide he tried there which was apparently not at all pleasant: 'I seemed sinking into annihilation … I do not think I shall die'.[15] As a result of the successful nitrous oxide experiment, Davy decides to take a larger dose five days later, a dose of 3 quarts (6 pints, 3.4 litres) from a silk bag. He describes it as:

> A fullness of the heart accompanied by loss of distinct sensation and of voluntary power, a feeling analogous to that produced in the first stage of intoxication.[16]

The next day, 17th April 1799, he breathes a dose larger yet: 4 quarts (8 pints, 4.5 litres). He reports that it induces,

> a highly pleasurable thrilling … the sense of muscular power became greater…[17]

Davy continues to frequently take nitrous oxide between May and December 1799, sometimes *five times a day* (with no less than 6 to 9 quarts each time).[18] On one of these days he discovers, whilst suffering from severe toothache, that when breathing nitrous oxide the,

> uneasiness was for a few minutes, swallowed up in pleasure.[19]

Davy writes of another anaesthetic occasion from nitrous oxide of the same period:

> [W]hen I had head-ache from indigestion, it was immediately removed by the effects of a large dose of gas…

But Davy's concern is not for the anaesthetic effects of nitrous oxide, as can be understood through the fact that its first use as such occurred only four decades later. Davy's concern was more metaphysical than medical:

> 'Sometimes I had feelings of intense intoxication … at other times, sublime emotions connected with highly vivid ideas…'[20]

He also writes that large doses of nitrous oxide are, 'superior in intensity to that occasioned by high intoxication from opium or alcohol'[21] revealing his use and familiarity with opium, a very common painkilling drug at the time – one to which Davy's friend Coleridge became painfully addicted (he famously referred to it as *the milk of paradise*),[22] and one that also had psychedelic-visionary properties, as conveyed so well by another of Davy's acquaintances, Thomas de Quincey.[23]

Davy is not content with the amounts of nitrous oxide he is taking. He wants more. On 26th December 1799 the intake of truly heroic doses of nitrous oxide begins. Davy's accomplice, the engineer James Watt, had designed an air-tight breathing box – aptly resembling somewhat a realm-transporting Tardis. The breathing box was installed in the Pneumatic Institution. On Boxing Day Davy steps inside. Now 80 quarts (90 litres) of nitrous oxide are pumped in over 75 minutes. Davy reports that:

> luminous points seemed frequently to pass before my eyes...[24]

As Davy steps out, he takes another 20 quarts from a silk bag. In his book of 1800, *Researches Chemical and Philosophical, Chiefly Concerning Nitrous Oxide*, Davy recounts what happened following the intake of these 100 quarts of nitrous oxide:

> A thrilling extending to the chest to the extremities was almost immediately produced. ... [My] visible impressions were dazzling and apparently magnified, I heard distinctly every sound in the room and was perfectly aware of my situation. By degrees as the pleasurable sensations increased I lost all connection with external things; trains of vivid visible images rapidly passed through my mind and were connected with words in such a manner, as to produce perceptions perfectly novel. I existed in a world of newly connected and newly modified ideas. I theorised .... My emotions were enthusiastic and sublime .... [W]ith the most intense belief and prophetic manner, I exclaimed to Dr. Kinglake, "Nothing exists but thoughts!—the universe is composed of impressions, ideas, pleasures and pains!"[25]

In Davy's private notes of the same event, his account is less inhibited:

> The sensations were superior to any I ever experienced. Inconceivably pleasurable .... I seemed to be a sublime being, newly created and superior to other mortals, I was indignant of

what they said of me and stalked majestically out of the laboratory to inform Dr Kinglake that nothing existed but thoughts.[26]

Davy continued using nitrous oxide, in his everyday life, writing in his book of 1800:

> I have often felt very great pleasure when breathing it alone, in darkness and silence, occupied only by ideal existence.[27]

Furthermore, in this unprecedented scientific and phenomenological book of 1800, Davy already writes of the *indescribability* of such psychedelic states, a notion of limitation that William James was to make common in his book a hundred years later, by the criterion of 'ineffability' for mystical states (that explicitly include those of nitrous oxide). Davy notes that:

> I have sometimes experienced from nitrous oxide, sensations similar to no others, and they have consequently been indescribable.[28]

Were a congenitally blind man to experience colours in a dream, he would not know that they were colours, let alone would he be able to describe them in any way but negatively (not sound, not taste, etc.) or analogically. So it is with ineffable psychedelic experiences for us: the novelty of such mentality overflows our linguistic containers. Davy noted this in his first book, but he would return to it later, using an insectoid analogy in his last book, as will be shown.

Though certain experiences were purportedly indescribable, Davy was wise to employ for a chapter in this initial book a number of Britain's finest writers so to gain as good a phenomenological description as was possible of the effects of the gas. These luminaries included Coleridge, Dr Roget (of later thesaurus fame), and poet-laureate-to-be, Robert Southey. In an enthusiastic letter to Davy, Southey described the gas in the following inspirational fashion:

> [Y]our gaseous oxide, which according to my notions of celestial enjoyment, must certainly constitute the atmosphere of the highest of all possible heavens.[29]

— — —

"Nothing exists but thoughts!" – it seems that Davy was swept to *idealism* through chemical means. Or rather, it seems that Davy received an intuition of what he had already considered intellectually – not only through his earlier readings of the subjective idealist Bishop Berkeley, but also through the concurrent German *Zeitgeist*. His brothers-in-thought, Coleridge and Wordsworth were captivated by, though not as yet well versed in, the idealism and related pantheism steaming out of the Continent, and Davy would have undoubtedly been immersed in the atmosphere of this exciting new philosophy. In fact, in one of Davy's notebooks of the time is a page entitled, 'System of Idealism',[30] after which is immediately written 'What philosophers call impressions, the world calls things'. After this, however, the meaning of his sentences become rather unintelligible, more convoluted than the densest of Hegelian passages. In fact, it would be quite reasonable to suppose that he was on nitrous oxide as he wrote it (or perhaps one should be on nitrous oxide as one reads it). In this context it is interesting to note that another prominent scientist-philosopher was also delivered to idealism of a Hegelian variety through the use of nitrous oxide. William James, almost a century after Davy's insight, writes:

> [The] effects of nitrous oxide gas-intoxication … have made me understand better than ever before both the strength and the weakness of Hegel's philosophy. I strongly urge others to repeat the experiment … an intense metaphysical illumination … . [Its] first result was to make peal through me with unutterable power the conviction that Hegelism was true after all…[31]

There are then a variety of types of idealism – including those of Berkeley, Kant, Fichte, Schelling, Hegel, Schopenhauer – with Kant's 'transcendental idealism' being the most influential. Though Davy and his poet friends endorsed idealism in Britain at the beginning of the nineteenth century, it would take another seventy years before British academic philosophers adopted it: the so-called 'British Idealism' of figures such as T. H. Green, B. Bosanquet, F. H. Bradley, and J. M. E. McTaggart. What is idealism? It is *idea-ism*: the view that mind is fundamental to all reality, rather than matter: "Nothing exists but thoughts!" One might say that for idealism, matter is a projection of the mind. Thus idealism is a viewpoint opposed to both materialism (that matter is fundamental, with mind being a product thereof), and dualism (that both matter and mind are fundamental). Before Davy first met Coleridge, in Bristol, Coleridge had spent time in Germany absorbing the new philosophy. Here he had also immersed himself in the metaphysics of Spinoza, arguably a special type of idealism.[32] In fact so involved was Coleridge in Spinoza that the government agent who was sent to spy on Coleridge and Wordsworth for possible traits of treason, concluded that the two were harmless but might have clocked on to him as they were constantly speaking of a 'Spy Nozy'.[33]

Now, in a notebook from the nitro days in Bristol, immediately after the poem 'On Breathing the Nitrous Oxide', Davy begins the poem 'The Spinosist'.[34] Of all of Davy's poems, this one appears to be the most important to him. As Sharon Ruston notes of it,

> He revised one poem ... at least four times, extending and developing it with each revision, and finally printing it anonymously twice within his lifetime. It is clear that this was a poem of which he was particularly proud and there is evidence that it was read aloud and circulated in manuscript among friends and acquaintances.[35]

What the continental philosophers had rationally theorized with regard to the mental depths of reality, the Cornish Davy had also, through the use of nitrous oxide, experimentally intuited. One can situate this within the general difference between Britain and the continent with regard to method, as Marcus Boon has thus situated it:

> The German Idealists themselves had little interest in this application of drugs. It was the British Romantics, empiricists at heart, who sought out experimental models for the study of the transcendental subject … . [T]hrough their philosophizing of their experiences with opium and nitrous oxide, [the Romantics] created "drugs" as we now know them.[36]

At that time, it was not stigma that dissuaded the German metaphysicians to avoid psychoactive chemical experimentation, it was rather the Enlightenment's crowning of the intellect that left other forms of intuitive consciousness in the shadows of importance. But there was a stigma, or moreover, a danger, in adopting Spinozism. Spinoza's bold, logical philosophy – one that rejected free will and the separation of body and soul, that advanced a moral relativism, and anticipated Nietzsche in seeing joy as a consequence of power, that saw sentience in all things (panpsychism), that dared to identify 'God' with 'Nature' – was a worldview not compatible with the ideology of Judeo-Christian power structures in place at the time. When F. H. Jacobi alleged that Enlightenment luminary G. E. Lessing was in later years secretly a Spinozist,[37] it triggered the *Pantheismusstreit*, the pantheism controversy of the late eighteenth century, that was to have hazardous occupational repercussion thence. Though Hegel said that one is 'either a Spinozist or not a philosopher at all',[38] it would generally be unwise to declare oneself a Spinozist at that time, and Davy certainly did not. However, it is enlightening to explore Davy's visions through the lens of Spinozism, a special case of examining psychedelic phenomenology through Spinozism that might provide new modes of thought for this psychedelic renaissance in which we find ourselves.

Let us then delve a little deeper into Spinoza and his system.[39] Baruch (later Benedict de) Spinoza was born in Amsterdam in 1632 and, like Davy, died young, in 1677. Though Dutch he was of the Sephardim: the Jews of the Iberian Peninsula who had fled the Portuguese Inquisition in the previous century. However, in his early twenties Spinoza was excommunicated by the Jewish community for his already-controversial views, and later condemned by the Church, having his work banned in 1674. In his influential *Dictionnaire Historique et Critique* published first in 1697, Calvinist Pierre Bayle referred to Spinozism as a 'most absurd and monstrous hypothesis',[40] precipitating the later, aforementioned pantheism controversy. Though Spinoza was offered a faculty position at Heidelberg University, he declined realizing that it would limit the expression of his thought. Instead, whilst immersed in the intellectual circles of Amsterdam, Spinoza would for the most spend his practical effort in grinding lenses.

Though ecclesiastico-politically repulsive, Spinozism was, and is, intellectually attractive. Echoing Davy's sentiments, though more explicitly, another most prominent scientist paid homage to Spinoza. As well as writing an endearing poem about the man, Einstein wrote that:

> I believe in Spinoza's God, who reveals himself in the harmony of all that exists…[41]

and:

> Spinoza is the greatest of modern philosophers, because he is the first philosopher who deals with the soul and the body as one, not as two separate things.[42]

So let us get to the substance of Spinoza's metaphysics, as given in his posthumous magnum opus, *Ethics*. Rather than admitting the two fundamental substances of reality as those of mind and matter, *à la* Descartes, Spinoza, using an Euclidianesque method, posited one substance alone – monism. This one substance is all that exists, and he calls it both Nature and God. In this sense, Spinozism can also be considered pantheism (as Spinoza's system was coined by Joseph Raphson in the late seventeenth century). This substance/Nature/God has an infinite number of *Attributes*: expressions, aspects, or versions, of this same substance. Though infinite in number, we humans only have access to two such Attributes, viz. Extension and Thought – essentially matter and mind. We have access to our consciousness, and we have access to the matter that seemingly constitutes our bodies and the universe around us. But Extension and its correlative Thought are not then two separate substances, but rather two different ways – Attributes – of viewing the same substance (God/Nature). Thus there can be no mind-body mental causation, no free will, because there are not two things that exist in a two-way cause-effect relationship. Elisabeth II cannot cause the motions of the current queen of the United Kingdom because they/she are/is one and the same – an epistemic qualitative difference but an ontological numerical identity. The neural correlates of consciousness express therefore a relationship of identity rather than one of causality. In relation to current neuroscience, especially with regard to understanding psychedelic phenomenology via brain activity, it is worth noting here that under Spinozism we would expect a perfect matter-mind correlation. This implies that even were the human neural correlates of consciousness completely mapped, the finding would not thereby evidence a materialist position. Mind-brain correlation merely indicates a part of the mind-matter relation. One does not adequately explain consciousness through neuroscience. Moreover, for Spinoza, it is not merely the brain and body but all of matter that correlates to mentality. Even a molecule has an element of mind, a position known as panpsychism.[43] This is an essentially logical position – as twentieth-century absolute idealist and panpsychist T. L. S. Sprigge has argued, 'the physical and the mental must be brought together everywhere or not at all'.[44] Now, for Spinoza, each Attribute has an infinite number of *Modes*, or modifications – so for instance the Attribute Extension has a Mode of magnesium, and the Attribute Thought has a Mode of magnanimity. Thus we have three main divisions of Spinozism: Substance, Attributes, and Modes, as represented in this figure:

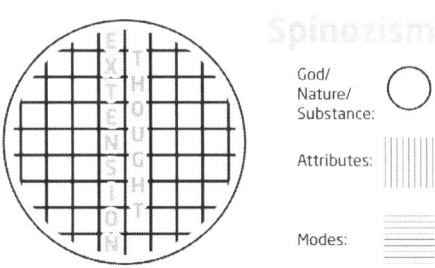

Spinoza's *Ethics* also includes two (of five) chapters on psychology which relates to his form of moral relativism which in this way can be seen as a precursor to Nietzsche. Spinoza's *conatus* – the inherent drive within all life to preservation and power – is akin to Nietzsche's will to power, and the emerging amoralism resultant therefrom is similar to Nietzsche's active nihilism.[45] In this conative-amoral connection, it is worth noting, with regard to the psychedelic renaissance vis-à-vis the law prohibiting psychedelic chemicals, that Spinoza advocated cognitive liberty:

> [W]hatever ... we judge to be good or to be profitable for the preservation of our being or the enjoyment of a rational life, we are permitted to take for our use and use in any way we may think proper; and absolutely, everyone is allowed by the highest right of nature to do that.[46]

But let us look more directly at Spinoza's metaphysics in relation to the psychedelic experience. To help frame the exploration, we can generalize three common categories of psychedelic experiences (though in truth such a taxonomy is vast). Firstly we have the indescribable, or to use William James' term for the mystical experience, 'ineffable' nature of the psychedelic experience. Before William James had used this word, Humphry Davy had claimed it for psychoactive experience, as quoted above and below. Secondly comes an experience that trades by many terms, one of which is 'cosmic consciousness', as used by Edward Carpenter,[47] R. M. Bucke,[48] and William James.[49] It is a mystical experience of being One with the universe, of thereby losing one's individuality – of losing *principium individuationis* – an experience often blissful, glorious, serene. By way of LSD especially, Alan Watts described the experience thus:

> [T]he individual discovers himself to be one continuous process with God, the Universe, with the Ground of Being, or whatever name he may use ... . [To] those who have known it, it is as real and overwhelming as falling in love.[50]

More concisely William James writes:

> In mystic states, we both become one with the Absolute and we become aware of our oneness.[51]

The third category that I shall use to generalize psychedelic experiences is that of otherworldly entity encounters. N,N-dimethyltryptamine, or simply DMT – inhaled pure, or taken as part of the Amazonian brew *ayahuasca* – is especially known for inducing this third category. Dr David Luke writes that this,

> psychedelic brew is taken because it gives rise to extraordinary mental phenomena ... perhaps most commonly, encounters with discarnate entities. When described by seemingly naïve DMT participants the entities encountered tend to vary in detail but often belong to one of a very few similar types ... [such as] mischievous shape-shifting elves, preying mantis alien brain surgeons and jewel-encrusted reptilian beings...[52]

Davy's alien encounters were of entities yet stranger – but before we travel to that third category, let us first look at the second – 'cosmic consciousness' – with respect to Davy through Spinoza.

Spinoza argues that we humans have three kinds of knowledge:[53] firstly there is 'opinion or imagination' which is simply our common daily sense- and language-based, vague understanding of the world. Secondly there is the more cognitive 'reason' through which we come to devise our science, mathematics, logic. Thirdly, and far less commonly, there is 'intuition' by which is meant an immediate, non-inferred grasping of a core essence of a reality. It is beyond the second kind of scientific knowledge, being more akin (but not identical) to what Kant conjectured as 'intellectual intuition',[54] and to what Bergson also referred to as 'intuition' or 'sympathy' as opposed to the rational 'intellect'.[55] It is an immersive, essential knowledge of the real – the rare insight of a poet, ever disturbed by the inadequacy of his description, having to rest content by the mere attempt at evocation.

It is as such immediate knowledge of the concrete rather than the second indirect knowledge of the abstract, an 'adequate knowledge of the essence of things'.[56] At its highest instantiation, Spinoza calls it *amor Dei intellectualis*, 'the intellectual love of God'. To attain this state, Spinoza tells us, is to attain the 'highest possible peace of mind, that is to say ... the highest joy'.[57] It is to intuit the concrete, absolute nature of reality in its non-temporal, i.e. *eternal*, form – i.e. to intuit *sub specie aeternitatis* (temporality being the means through which the mere two Attributes of Extension and Thought are manifest). It is love, according to Spinoza, because it is joy with the knowledge of its cause. Through this state, God/Nature, because it is not essentially separate from us, attains self-love: it is the means by which core reality comes to love itself through self-consciousness – in other words, a cosmic consciousness. In Spinoza's words:

> The intellectual love of the mind towards God is the very love with which He loves Himself, not in so far as He is infinite, but in so far as He can be manifested through the essence of the human mind, considered under the form of eternity ... . This love or blessedness is called glory in the sacred writings...[58]

Such a glorious state of Nature achieved through oneself was one sought by many Romantics, Davy being no exception. In a notebook entry dated to his nitrous years, he writes:

> To day for the first time in my life I have had a distinct sympathy with nature ... . Every[thing] seemed alive & myself part of the series of visible impressions. I should have felt pain in tearing a leaf from one of the trees – deeply & intimately connected are all our ideas of motion & life...[59]

In Davy's final book, *Consolations*, he too writes of such unitive states, now more opium-induced and still poetically evocative of Spinoza's *amor Dei*:

> I saw in all the powers of matter the instruments of the Deity; the sunbeams, the breath of the zephyr … . I saw love as the creative principle in the material world, and this love only as a Divine attribute … . Then, my own mind, I felt connected … a thirst for immortality.[60]

This was placed in the Fourth Dialogue of the *Consolations*. The First Dialogue, 'The Vision', is, it is fair to say, one of the earliest and one of the greatest 'trip reports' in the psychedelic canon, despite its being relatively unknown. The word 'vision' was often used in this period to refer to aesthetic opium experiences. In this chapter, Davy, as protagonist Philalethes, describes a vision he experiences as he falls into a trance state whilst resting in the Colosseum in Rome, flooded within moonshine. He comes to be guided by an alien spirit – the 'Genius' – through the history of Earth, seeing the progress of mankind from its beast-like beginnings through the epochs. That a few superior humans are pivotal to progress is often emphasized, such as King Alfred and Peter the Great (he does not explicitly name himself). The protagonist now finds himself in a dark cave. Then, in Platonic splendour, 'a bright and rosy light broke into this cave … above all was bright and illuminated with glory'.[61] He rises now above the planet into space, past the planets, beyond the solar system. He is then introduced to different alien, spiritual civilizations and their subjects in a style supremely psychedelic. We here meet a passage that combines both the second and third categories of psychedelic experience, cosmic consciousness with otherworldly encounters, with seemingly Spinozist overtones. The Genius conveys the common highest state of certain ethereal minds or (using a term commonly employed by Bruno and Leibniz) monads:

> There is one sentiment or passion which the monad or spiritual essence carries with it into all its stages of being, and which in these happy and elevated creatures [cometary fire-orb beings] is continually exalted: the love of knowledge or of intellectual power, which is, in fact, in its ultimate and most perfect

development the love of infinite wisdom and unbounded power, or the love of God. ... [At] the moment of death [it] is felt by the conscious being ... . [We solar beings] feel the personal presence of that supreme Deity which only you imagine; to you belongs faith, to us knowledge; and our greatest delight results from the conviction that we are lights kindled by His light and that we belong to His substance.[62]

We now move from the second category of psychedelic experience to the third: otherworldly entity encounters. Though sounding somewhat mystical with his *amor dei intellectualis*, Spinoza was sceptical, at the least, of the existence of ghosts, as certain correspondence shows.[63] However, he accepted the reality of revelation,[64] and we can consider, through his metaphysics, the possibility of the veridicality of visions of otherworldly entities. As shown, we humans have access to only two Attributes of Substance/Nature/God: Extension and Thought, matter and mind. The number of the Attributes of reality, however, is infinite. Would it be possible, under the Spinozist system, for a human to access, enter, another Attribute? It is barely possible for a human to conceive another Attribute outside of matter and mind, as it is impossible for a beetle to conceive of the reality of the galaxy in which it exists. But Frederick Pollock writes that such inhuman access is not impossible for Spinozism:

> Spinoza ... thought it possible that new Attributes might become known to us by revelation; for in one place ... he speaks of Thought and Extension as the only Attributes *as yet* known to us.[65]

Such revelatory knowledge would be a new state of existence. Moreover, to follow Davy in the bold conjectures that emanated from his noetic visions, would it be possible for a sentient being to primarily exist through mind and through a non-spatial Attribute? Davy thought so: in a letter of 1804, during his time as celebrated professor of chemistry in London, Davy writes:

> We are masters of the earth, but perhaps we are slaves of some great and unknown beings. The fly that we crush with our finger … has no knowledge of man, and no consciousness of his superiority. … There may be beings – thinking beings, near us, surrounding us, which we do not perceive, which we can never imagine. We know very little …[66]

Repeatedly throughout his life, Davy seems to have had such intuitions, the balance of their endogenous to exogenous causation unknown. Later in 1821, a year after he was elected President of the Royal Society, he writes of another vision:

> It seemed as if I was entering *a new state of existence* … I seemed in communication with some intelligent being … I hoped to be, ultimately, in a world of intellectual light…[67]

Two years prior, Davy recounts another similar otherworldly encounter, one that was indubitably to inspire his later account in *Consolations*.[68] In his notebook, Davy writes:

> One moonlit night … I was walking in the Colosseum full of sublime thoughts … when of a sudden I saw a bright mist in one of the arcades, so luminous that I thought a person must be advancing with a light. … [A] voice, distinct, but like that of a flute, said, "I am one of the Roman deities! You disbelieve all the ancient opinions, as dreams and fables; nevertheless they are founded in truth. Before the existence of man, and some time after, a race of beings who are independent of respiration and air occasionally dwelt on the globe … In the early stage of society we condescended to instruct man …"[69]

Davy did not consider experiences such as these to be nothing but hallucination. If materialism were true, then both cosmic consciousness and otherworldly encounters would be nothing more than tricks of the material brain. But in Spinozism matter is not fundamental – it is not substance – but one of an infinity of equal Attributes. Davy himself rails against materialism, echoing Leibniz's Mill[70] in *Consolations* that:

> I can never believe that any division, or refinement, or subtilisation, or juxtaposition, or arrangement of the particles of matter, can give to them sensibility; or that [sentient] intelligence can result from combinations of insensate and brute atoms.[71]

This was written in 1829, and today materialism, now physicalism, still faces this hard problem of consciousness – a problem that can really be seen as falsification of materialism, unless hopes are placed in the faith that is 'promissory materialism', as Karl Popper snubs it.[72] So it would be presumptive to reduce the ethereal experiences Davy had to hallucinations produced by the brain when we do not understand how the brain produces consciousness at all, despite correlation. Davy himself considered the philosophical positions laid out in *Consolations* to be of utmost importance to his worldview, as mentioned – and with regard to the existence of the beings of his visions, he therein allows for their possibility:

> [In] other systems beings of a superior nature, under the influence of a divine will, may act nobler parts. We know from sacred writings that there are intelligences of a higher nature than man …. [Such] seraphic intelligences may inhabit these [empyrean] systems and may be ministers of the eternal mind…[73]

Behind the dialogue of his visionary guide, Davy can be more candid:

> Spiritual natures are eternal and indivisible, but their modes of being are as infinitely varied as the forms of matter. They have no relation to space, and, in their transitions, no dependence upon time, so that they can pass from one part of the universe to another by laws entirely independent of their motion …. [T]hey are, in fact, parts more or less inferior of the infinite mind…[74]

After this visionary speculation, Davy goes into detail describing a crystalloid alien cityscape, a description that two centuries on is not dated but entirely fitting of modern science fiction:

> I saw below me a surface infinitely diversified, something like that of an immense glacier covered with large columnar masses, which appeared as if formed of glass, and from which were suspended rounded forms of various sizes, which, if they had not been transparent, I might have supposed to be fruit. ... [M]asses of bright blue ice, streams of the richest tint of rose colour or purple ... immense [living] masses ... I saw with great surprise that they moved from place to place by six extremely thin membranes which they used as wings...[75]

The first chapter of *Consolations* teem with such alien visions, with analysis thereof set in the next and last chapters. Though beautifully conveyed, Davy emphasized, as he had written of nitrous oxide experiences, that many if not most of these unworldly experiences were ultimately indescribable (as per the first category of psychedelic experience). In the book Davy now expresses this limitation of expressing the psychedelic state through insectoid analogy:

> You are now in a state in which a fly would be whose microscopic eye was changed to one similar to that of man; and you are wholly unable to associate what you now see with your former knowledge.[76]

That is, what it is like to be a fly being a man is analogous to what it is like to be a man tripping psychedelic. In relation to the mysteries of understanding consciousness here, it should be noted that philosopher Thomas Nagel famously asked, 'What is it like to be a bat?'[77] – with the intention of emphasizing the fact that a complete physical account of an animal's body and brain will not yield a full understanding of the subjective experience which that organism may have. This is a point already made by Davy, as quoted above. Nagel later acknowledges[78] that even his use of the interrogative, 'What is it like…' is anticipated in the 'semi-Spinozistic'[79] idealist T. L. S. Sprigge,[80] and before him used by the behaviourist B. A. Farrell.[81] Interestingly we come full circle here: Davy's use of the insect analogy to convey the ineffability of *what it is like* to experience opium-induced visions, is mirrored in the phrase's first use by Farrell. Farrell asked in his 1950 article 'Experience':

1. "I wonder what it would be like to be an opium smoker."
2. "I wonder what it would be like to be, and hear like, a bat."[82]

What Davy understood was that the two questions could be almost equated: what it is like to be another creature can *be* what it is like to be an opium smoker. That is, Davy understood that by chemical means, other states of consciousness, nay, other states of existence, can be attained. Thus though reason yields theoretical metaphysics, psychedelics yield practical metaphysics – therefore to be a genuine mind researcher one must brave hell and soar angelic. Such flights were taken, and their value realized, by the western world's very first scientific psychonaut: Penzance's son of genius, Sir Humphry Davy.

The Spinosist

Lo o'er the earth the kindling spirits pour
The seeds of life that bounteous nature gives. —
The liquid dew becomes the rosy flower
The sordid dust awakes & moves & lives. —
All, All is change, the renovated forms
Of ancient things arise & live again.
The light of suns the angry breath of storms
The everlasting motions of the main
Are but the engines of that powerful will. —
The eternal link of thoughts where form resolves
Has ever acted & is acting still
Whilst age round age & world round world revolves.
Linked to the whole the human mind displays
No sameness & no deep identity [divine]
Changeful as the surface of the seas
Impressible as is the blue moving sky
[To scattered thoughts some unknown laws are given
By which they join and move in circling life. —]
Being of aggregate the power of love
Gives it the joy of moments bids it rise
In the wild forms of mortal things to move
Fix'd to the earth below the eternal skies
To breath the ether; & to feel the form
Of orbed beauty through its organs thrill
To press the limbs of life with rapture warm
And drink of transport from a living rill. —
To view the heavens with morning radiance bright
Majestic mingling with the ocean blue. —
[Filled by a thousand silver streams
& played upon by ten thousand cloudless breezes]
To view the forests green the mountains white

The peopled plains of rich and varied hue. —
To feel the social flame to give to man
Ten thousand signs of burning energy,
The nothingness of human words to scan
The nothingness of human things cares to fly. —
To live in forests mingled with [the whole]
Of natures forms, to feel the breezes play
O'er the parched forebrow to see the planets roll
O'er their grey head their life diffusing ray
To die in agony & In many days
To give to Nature all her stolen powers
Etherial fire to feed the solar rays
Etherial dew to feed the earth in showers.

(RI, HD/34/c, pp. 7–10)

Acknowledgements

My gratitude goes to Mike Jay for providing initial reading material, avenues of exploration, and for his review of a draft of this essay; to Sharon Ruston for providing me with reading material and routes to examine; to Jane Harrison of the Royal Institution for providing me with certain copies of Davy's notebooks; to the conference Beyond Psychedelics and to the Penzance Literary Festival for hosting my talk on this topic which resulted in this text; to Morrab Library in Penzance for providing some early texts of Davy's (and Davy's own chair), and to the Univeresity of Exeter for funding the excursions.

Notes

1. *The Prelude*, V, 595–598; Wordsworth, p. 674.
2. In Humphry Osmond's letter to Aldous Huxley, 1956.
3. See Pollan, 2018, Pref.
4. Boyle and Hooke dallied with psychoactive drugs, notably cannabis, but were not as methodological, as *scientific* as Davy in this sense. Thanks to Chris Bennett for bringing to my attention the two Roberts in this respect. In his wish list of future human discoveries, Boyle includes (in the 1660s): 'Potent Druggs to alter or Exalt Imagination, Waking, Memory, and other functions, and appease pain, procure innocent sleep, harmless dreams, etc.' (Online: https://blogs.royalsociety.org/history-of-science/2010/08/27/robert-boyle-list/ [accessed 9th July 2018].)
5. 'Psychonaut', coined by Ernst Jünger (1970), means a person who explores the mind via psychoactive chemicals.
6. Though the way is shown today by inspired writers such as Molly Lefebure, Richard Holmes, Sharon Ruston, and Mike Jay – the last two of whom I am grateful for guidance at the start of this trip, and to the last also for the end.
7. See for instance the letter to his wife dated 1827-10-02 (RI, HD/25/62). Available online at: http://davy-letters.org.uk. Note that the code in brackets in the first sentence is a reference to the Humphry Davy material held at the Royal Institution. I hereby thank the Royal Institution for providing me with certain copies of Davy's notebooks.
8. Letter to Poole, February 1829. See Hartley, 1972, p. 147.
9. See Lefebure, 1990, p. 95.
10. As indicated in his notebook of 1795 – See Hartley, 1972, pp. 11-12.
11. See for instance his 'Prospectus of my Theory of Mind', in the notebook of 1796 (RI, HD/13/f, pp. 55–58).
12. 1802 letter to his mother, quoted in Hartley, 1972, p. 11.
13. Who was son to the engineer James Watt.
14. Jay, p. 162.
15. See Hartley, 1972, p. 28.
16. Hartley, p. 27.
17. Ibid.
18. Davy, 1800, p. 462.
19. Davy, 1800, p. 465.
20. Davy, 1800, p. 462.
21. Davy, 1800, p. 484.
22. Coleridge, *Kubla Khan*.
23. See de Quincey's *Confessions of an English Opium Eater*.
24. Davy, 1800, p. 487.

25	Davy, 1800, p. 488–9.
26	Quoted in Holmes, 2009, p. 270.
27	Davy, 1800, p. 491.
28	Davy, 1800, p. 405.
29	August 1799. Quoted from Green, 2016, p. 54.
30	RI, HD/13/d, p. 18. With thanks once more to the Royal Institution.
31	*Mind*, 1882, Vol. 7.
32	See for example Murray, 1896.
33	Coleridge, 1817/2014, Ch. X, p. 133.
34	RI, HD/13/c, pp. 7–10. Note that above the title 'The Spinosist', above some crossed out initial lines, stands the alternative title 'The Life of the Spinosist'.
35	Ruston, in: Hagen and Vibe Skagen (eds.), 2013, pp. 77–78.
36	Boon, p. 92.
37	For details, see for instance Gerrish, 1987.
38	Hegel, Pt. 3, §2, ch. 1, A2, p. 283.
39	For a more detailed examination of Spinozism in relation to the psychedelic experience, especially that induced by 5-MeO-DMT, see my chapter 'The White Sun of Substance: Spinozism and the Psychedelic *amor Dei Intellectualis*', in: Hauskeller and Sjöstedt-Hughes (eds.), 2022.
40	Vol. III, p. 287.
41	4th April 1929, Einstein cable to Rabbi Herbert S. Goldstein.
42	From an interview published in G. S. Viereck's book *Glimpses of the Great* (1930).
43	See the first chapter in this book.
44	1977, p. 443.
45	For Nietzsche's differing uses of 'nihilism', see Sjöstedt-Hughes, 2009.
46	Spinoza, 1677/2001: *Ethics*, 4P, Appx §8, p. 218.
47	Carpenter, 1892.
48	From his 1901 book, *Cosmic Consciousness: A Study in the Evolution of the Human Mind*. One section of in this psychiatrist's book is on Spinoza in relation to cosmic consciousness (Pt. V, ch. 9, pp. 151–153).
49	James, 1902/1985, p. 398. The term 'eternal consciousness' had been used in the decades prior to this by the British Idealists (see Sprigge, 2006).
50	'Psychedelics and Religious Experience', *California Law Review*, 56:1, January 1968, p. 74. Also reprinted as Appendix to Watts, 2013.
51	James, 1902/1985, p. 419.
52	Luke, p. 85.
53	Spinoza, 1677/2001: *Ethics*, 2P40s2, p. 80.

54	See *Critique of Pure Reason*, B145, p. 253.
55	See for instance ch. II of *Creative Evolution*.
56	Spinoza, 1677/2001: *Ethics*, 5P25d, p. 245.
57	Spinoza, 1677/2001: *Ethics*, 5P32d, p. 248.
58	Spinoza, 1677/2001: *Ethics*, 5P36, p. 250.
59	RI, HD/13/d, 9–10 (11 July 1800 entry).
60	Davy, 1830/2005, Dialogue Four, p. 78.
61	Davy, 1830/2005, D1, p. 20.
62	Davy, 1830/2005, D1, p. 25.
63	See Pollock, pp. 59–61.
64	See Pollock, pp. 357–368.
65	Pollock, p. 355.
66	To William Clayfield (botanist, businessman), 21st October 1804. Online at: http://davy-letters.org.uk.
67	Quoted in Lefebure, 1986, p. 58. My italics.
68	*Consolations* was also the result of a planned joint epic with Coleridge to be called *Moses* (see Lefebure, 1990, p. 102); and, Mike Jay suggests in personal correspondence, based on *The Ruins* by C. F. Volney.
69	Notebook entry dated 9th November 1819. See Lefebure, 1990, pp. 105–6.
70	Leibniz, 1989, p. 215 (in the *Monadology* [1714]): 'perception … is inexplicable in terms of mechanical reasons, that is through shapes and motions. If we imagine a machine whose structure makes it think … [and imagine] we could enter into it, as one enters a mill. Assuming that, when inspecting its interior, we will find parts that push one another, and we will never find anything to explain a perception.'
71	Davy, 1830/2005, 4D, pp. 73–4.
72	Popper and Eccles, Part I (Popper), ch. P3, §26, pp. 96–98.
73	Davy, 1830/2005, 6D, p. 98.
74	Davy, 1830/2005, 1D, p. 20.
75	Ibid., p. 21.
76	Ibid., p. 22.
77	Nagel, 1974.
78	Nagel, 1986, p. 15, fn. 2: 'When I wrote I hadn't read Sprigge and had forgotten Farrell.'
79	Sprigge, 1983, p. 158.
80	Sprigge and Montefiore, 1971, p. 167.
81	Farrell, 1950.
82	Ibid., p. 183.

Deeper than Depth
N-Dimensional Space and Sentience

The waking have one common world [*koinos kosmos*], but the sleeping turn aside each into a world of their own [*idios kosmos*].[1]
— Heraclitus

The inquiry into the relation between 'mind' and 'matter' too often stops at the status of profound mystery because those very terms are poorly understood. What is understood is that the solution to the mystery requires revolutionary thought, since present concepts do not provide sufficient scope through which to see the end of this cosmic riddle. We must therefore extend our vision and experiment with ocular instruments beyond those found in the traditional philosopher's observatory. To gain a greater gaze into this outer space we will analyse space itself, fracturing it into three varieties and raising it beyond three dimensions. What follows is a playful trip of radical speculation through hyperspace.

1. Mind, Matter, and Space
2. The Varieties of Space
3. The Dimensions of Space and Sentience

1. Mind, Matter, and Space

From the Cartesian legacy, it is often assumed that matter is spatial (extensive) and mind, or sentience,[2] is non-spatial (inextensive). Descartes writes for instance that:

> [Although] I possess a body with which I am very intimately conjoined, yet because, on the one side, I have a clear and distinct idea of myself inasmuch as *I am only a thinking [sentient] and unextended thing*, and as, on the other, I possess a distinct idea of body, inasmuch as *it is only an extended [spatial] and unthinking thing*, it is certain that this I is entirely and absolutely distinct from my body, and can exist without it.[3]

This dichotomy of spatial-matter and nonspatial-mind conveys Descartes' dualism, and is no doubt partly responsible for the cataclysmic scientific view of nature as merely mechanical, insentient – despite the fact that it was presented by the Catholic Descartes to substantiate the religious soul perspective.[4]

Thus we glimpse in passing the *prima facie* paradoxical influence of the Church upon Western science. Neither dualism nor scientific mechanism comes close to explaining the mind-matter relation, so let us question their common basis: is mind aspatial, matter spatial? William James, a pioneer of philosophic-psychedelic exploration, criticized the Cartesian assumption:

> Descartes for the first time defined thought as the absolutely unextended … . But to argue … that experience is absolutely inextensive seems to me little short of absurd.[5]

In an earlier paper, 'The Spatial Quale', James had grounded such a view, speaking of the existence of spatial properties not only without but within imagination:

> The primary [visual] sensation is a simple vastness, a teeming muchness. The perception of positions within it results from sub-dividing it. The measurement of distances and directions comes later still.[6]

If we close our eyes and imagine two triangles next to each other, we can speak of their spatial properties – such as each having three sides, angles that sum 180°, that one triangle may be to the left of, and above, the other, and vice versa, their relative proximity, boundaries and topological features, their relative sizes, etc. These properties are perhaps often not as stable as would be two triangles perceived with eyes open, yet they are spatial properties regardless of such stable durability.[7]

Thus we have here two types of space, correlated yet not *prima facie* identical. Bertrand Russell expresses such a dichotomy when he writes that:

> [P]ercepts are not identical with material objects, and the relation of perceptual to physical space is not identity.[8]

2. The Varieties of Space

Thus we are led to posit the reality of *twofold space*: physical space and sentient space. This pair can also, respectively, be referred to as extrinsic and intrinsic space, or objective and subjective space. Unfortunately all of these labels bear metaphysical connotations that can interfere with a proper understanding of their essences and relation – as we shall come to understand (e.g. physical space is perceived as such within our subjective space, and sentient space may not be merely intrinsic). But for now we note the relation of this general twofold space to the Herclitus epigraph above where sentient space refers to the *idios kosmos*, physical space to our shared *koinos kosmos*. Sentient space not only includes that of imagination, but also that of hypnagogia, psychedeliscapes, and the space of dreams. Russell's teacher and later colleague and friend, Alfred North Whitehead, also spoke implicitly of this distinctive *idios kosmos*:

> The distinction between the dream-world and nature is, that the space-time of the dream-world cannot conjoin with the scheme of the space-time of nature, as constituted by any part of nature. The dream-world is nowhere at no time, though it has a dream-time and dream-space of its own.[9]

We must distinguish then physical from sentient space. Sentient space, however, ramifies into more than *visual space*.[10] We also have the sense of space related to our bodies: *somatic space*.

Maurice Merleau-Ponty distinguishes somatic sentient space from physical space, and argues that the distinction lies in the fact that the latter is indirectly intellectualized in terms of relations or positions to objective geometric coordinates whereas the former is directly felt in terms of a top-down 'global awareness' of the situationally-determined location of one's bodily parts:

> [My] body's spatiality is not, like the spatiality of external objects or of "spatial sensations," a positional spatiality; rather it is a situational spatiality. ... When the word "here" is applied to my body, it does not designate a determinate position in relation to other positions or in relation to external coordinates. It designates the installation of the first coordinates, the anchoring of the active body in an object, and the situation of the body confronted with its tasks. Bodily space can be distinguished from external space and it can envelope its parts rather than laying them out side by side...[11]

William James had earlier issued an equivalent point: 'the feeling arising from the excitement of any extended part of the body is felt as extended',[12] yet Merleau-Ponty offers a more thorough somatic phenomenology, for instance adding an Alice in Wonderland Syndrome phenomenological case:

> [If] I can in general sense the space of my body as enormous or as tiny despite the evidence of my senses, this is because there is an affective presence and extension of which objective spatiality is neither the sufficient condition … nor even the necessary condition…[13]

The haptic sense, touch, is a part of somatic space, and one that lends itself especially to the feeling of the real: 'it is our sense of touch that gives our sense of "reality"',[14] Russell claims. Moreover, the gustatory sense, i.e. taste, is also, arguably,[15] a type of touch (by the tongue) – one that yields more data (flavour) than does standard skin-based touch. As to whether the olfactory, auditory, and other senses,[16] involve spatiality is a question that I shall not address here (note that James argues that *all* senses are spatial).[17] It is sufficient for our purposes to show that there *exist* perceptual spaces distinct from extrinsic, physical space.

Further: there are spaces and spatial properties which we can *conceptualize* yet not visualize nor (at least directly) feel somatically. For instance, we can easily conceptualize four dimensional space by simply adding an axis w, to the traditional three – x, y, z – and thus create a hypothetical hyperspace[18] that can be developed through algebraic geometry. However, such a conceptual space is not identical to a visual space: though a fourth dimension orthogonal (right-angled) to our traditional three can be *conceived*, it is very difficult (to say the least) to *visualize* this directly. The distinction between conceptual and visual space is accentuated further if we were to posit a myriad of dimensions. As conceptual spaces often indicate possibility rather than actuality (i.e. physical space), we are led to assert *threefold space*: physical, perceptual, and conceptual. This tristinction is further made necessary when we consider the fact that there can exist conceptual spaces which we have never considered. As undiscovered universals they have an objective existence with the ontic status of possibility rather than actuality, as they exist not in our sentient minds and thus not in our physical brains. This threefold space is illustrated in *Figure 1*.

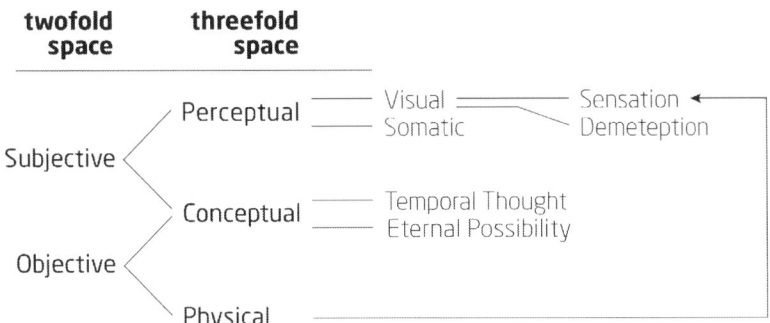

Figure 1

A further ramification will be noted here: visual perception itself takes may forms. Its major division is that between the physical veridical and non-veridical, i.e. between the direct ocular sensation of the extrinsic world ('seeing'), and with 'demeteption':[19] imagination, episodic memory, dreams, hypnagogia, hallucination, psychedelic experience, etc. The direct visual perception of extrinsic space is a mostly[20] subjective *representation* of the actual objective physical space – we must differentiate the representation from the represented here. And we must also note that our human representation of extrinsic space is just that: human (not absolute).

What objective, physical space actually *is* is itself an ongoing vast enquiry, as we shall see. Our understanding of it has shifted paradigmatically from Plato's view of it as somewhat of a container,[21] a view more distinctly emphasized as such by Lucretius, who saw space (the 'void') as distinct from matter ('body'). In the first century BC, Lucretius writes:

> All nature, as it is in itself, consists
> Of two things: there are bodies and there is void
> In which these bodies are and through which they move.[22]

Today this *dualism* between matter and space has been generally effaced by considering space (or, Minkowski-Einstein spacetime) as itself a form of matter (as anticipated by Leibniz).[23] Physicist Carlo Rovelli (inspired by LSD to investigate the physics of space and time)[24] for instance, writes that 'Spacetime is a physical object like an electron.'[25] And this physical object '[s]pacetime *is* the gravitational field'.[26] Further, as with all physical objects, spacetime itself is believed by certain physicists to exhibit wave-particle duality, thus the search for the graviton particle to complement the gravitational field. Of course, spacetime as a physical object is of a different sort to that of what we generally consider to be physical objects, which take their form instead from electromagnetic and nuclear forces. But we must always urge caution with regard to current scientific hypotheses due to *pessimistic induction*: we see physics changing constantly, so we must not expect that the current state of knowledge therein is final. Moreover, the current state of physics is not some harmonious unity but rather an arena of competing theories, with Rovelli's preferred quantum gravity theory, for instance, competing against string theories. We should speak not of one physics but of "physicses", my precious. But it is sufficient here simply to emphasize the threefold analytic distinction amongst perceptual space, conceptual space, and physical space – whatever physical space may be.[27] It should also be emphasized that any unified theory in physics that does not factor sentience can never be a theory of everything.

Now, this threefold analysis raises a question: How are these varieties of space related? Let us here approach this question with a twofold space – visual and physical space, *idios* and *koinos kosmos* – which will be a journey via hyperspace into the blackhole that is the mind-matter problem.

> [T]here can be infinitely many spaces and, hence, worlds, such that between them and ours there is no distance.[28]
> – Leibniz

3. The Dimensions of Space and Sentience

I close my eyes and imagine a blue equilateral triangle. This triangle exists as such, as a demetept, and has an endo-physical correlate:[29] certain activity in the occipital lobe of my brain, for instance. This latter is an example of the so-called neural correlates of consciousness.[30] The correlation presents the problem (not the answer) to the question of how visual and physical space relate. What are options[31] to resolve this relation?:

i. *Substance Dualism*: the triangle and the neural correlates are separate substances, not dependent on each other.
ii. *Emergentism*: the triangle emerges from the neural correlates.
iii. *Idealism*: the neural correlates emerge from the mind.
iv. *Psycho-neural Identity Theory*: the triangle *is* the neural correlates.
v. *More-Broad-Smythies Theory*: the triangle and the neural correlates are both cross-sections of a deeper hyperspace.

3:i – Substance Dualism

Let us briefly venture through these options. We start by aiming at substance dualism (with blunderbuss not sniper): that the mind and the body are separate substances. There do exist nuanced arguments for the reality of dualism, though it is considered more a religious than intellectual stance. Dualism makes the existence of the neural correlates somewhat superfluous: why would a blue triangle have neural correlates? More generally, what would be the purpose of any of the purported neural correlates of consciousness? If a soul substance could move a body, why act first on the brain rather than directly on the muscles? Why would an independent soul stick to one body alone? Why could a soul not directly move surrounding objects rather than the body alone – i.e. instigate telekinesis? Why can a soul not be empirically detected? If dualism is fused with metempsychosis, why can we not recall former lives? If dualism is not fused with metempsychosis, how are souls produced with the foetus or infant? Do all organisms have souls (including insects, plants and fungi), and if not what is the criterion for exclusion? Where dwell the souls without bodies? Why is there no known causal force between a soul and a body? How could a non-physical soul interact with (push or pull) a physical body without transgressing the law of conservation of energy? These and other such basic questions have pushed people away from dualism to find more plausible solutions to the relation between mind and matter. But crucially for us, Descartes' dualism does not even allow for the spatiality, extension, of the mental. In line with James' point above, this appears contrary to the plain evidence of our imaginations. In the words of neurophilosopher John R. Smythies:

> [The] basic premiss of Cartesian Dualism – that mental events lack extension in space – is clearly incompatible with the evidence from introspectionist psychology.[32]

Thus there is no possible solution to question of how visual and physical space relate in Cartesian dualism because the former is ultimately denied.

3:ii – Emergentism

Emergentism is the view that the mind emerges from the body, that, in our case, the triangle emerges from its neural correlates. This, in its general form, is arguably the prevalent view today amongst those in consciousness studies – though it was also prevalent a century ago with the so-called 'British Emergentists'.[33] There are two essential problems with emergentism: upward and downward causation. 'Upward causation' refers to emergence itself: by which laws of nature does a blue equilateral triangle emerge from the fleshy activity of the brain? How do the impulses, waves of ions, through the axons and dendrites (branches) of neurons, and the release and reception of neuromodulators (certain molecules) between synapses (neural extremities), and other such physical movements, then produce – make emerge – a perceived triangle? There are no such known laws in science that bridge the body to the mind, no such 'bridge laws' (or, 'transordinal laws/nomology').[34] This renders emergentism non-scientific, despite the fact that many scientists unwittingly endorse it. In addition to having no explanatory bridge *laws* between the bodily motion and mentality, there are no observable *causal lines* from one to the other. One cannot trace a motion to an emotion, and one cannot 'zoom' into an emotion to find a motion. One could diachronically trace the emergence of a hurricane to the flap of a butterfly's wing, and one could synchronically zoom into a hurricane to see how it emerges from the motions of its molecules; but one could not diachronically trace the emergence of an imagined triangle from neurological activity nor could one synchronically zoom into an imagined triangle to find neurological activity in its lines and angles. If one responds that it is not a matter of emergence but of constitution, then one has rejected emergentism in favour of psycho-neural identity theory, which we shall soon expose.

There are many more problems with such 'upward causation', but there are problems further still with the 'downward causation' posited in emergentism. The important form of downward causation here is *mental causation*, of which 'free will' is a subform.[35] There are many varieties of mental causation,[36] such as a desire to walking, a calculation to pencilling, and a train of consequential thoughts – from mind to body, or from mind to mind. If one rejects mental causation one is deemed an 'epiphenomenalist',[37] and this is a label that most emergentists seek to avoid. Why? One logical reason is given by the philosopher Friedrich Paulsen:

> If thought can be the effect of movements, there is no reason whatever why a movement should not be the effect of a thought.[38]

There are also evolutionary reasons for maintaining mental causation, as expounded for instance, by F. H. Bradley[39] and Karl Popper:[40] If mentality has no power at all, why has it evolved and maintained itself not only in humans but presumably in the multiplicity of other species? Though there may be spandrels (useless evolved phenomena), to claim that mentality itself, the essence of *who we are*, is a spandrel appears absurd. It would be to claim that our conscious perception and our intelligence played no role in our individual or collective lives. For such reasons, emergentists want to endorse mental causation.[41] However, to show that that which has emerged can also have an effect upon that from which it emerged has played circular havoc with the very idea of emergentism.[42] For these and other reasons,[43] it is better that we submerge the idea and sail on to other mind-matter theories. To claim that an imagined triangle emerges from physiological activity is not to provide an answer but merely to postpone the question: *How* does it 'emerge'? A viable answer requires not only the presentation of physiological machinations but the physiological-to-phenomenological process. Hence neuroscience alone cannot answer this issue. (Furthermore, to maintain downward causation, we would also require an explanation of phenomenological-to-physiological processes.) Emergentism cannot resolve the question as to the relation between physical and visual space[44] – *the twofold space interface problem.*

3:iii – Idealism

There are a variety of versions of idealism which in its basic meaning is the belief that the mind creates the world we perceive. In its extreme form, this presents *solipsism*: that *only* the mind exists, all else being non-veridical, illusion. But in its more developed form, such as that from Immanuel Kant, it is the idea that though the mind does produce the phenomena we perceive, there is nonetheless a reality separate from us underlying in part those phenomena: viz. the world-in-itself – a world *completely* unknown to us as our representations of it are always only human interpretations. Even space, time, and causality are, for this idealism, mere categories of our mind that thus do not exist outside our minds. Now there is much to value in idealism, and I can only here offer the sparsest critique of a theory that in fairness requires for such a critique a lifetime's analysis. Concerning our example, there is no twofold space because there is no physical space: physical space can only ever be perceptual space. Therefore there is no twofold space interface problem. Rather than a solution to the problem, idealism seems to offer a dissolution of the problem – at least, at a first glance. Idealism would still need to differentiate what appears as physical space from what appears as visual space, and explain the relation between the two. Kant's transcendental idealism explains this relation by arguing that space (and time) are pure forms of intuition that exist in our minds as molds, as it were, that shape incoming sensations spatially and temporally. If there are no (*a posteriori*) sensations (molded *a priori* into spatial forms), then there still remain those *a priori* forms of intuition.[45] Put more primitively, our minds are spatial molds that when filled present physical space and when empty present imaginary space.

We cannot get into the (mass) detail of transcendental idealism here, but we note that that which correlates to an imagined triangle (physiological activity) is itself also a mere apparent phenomena, but in-itself something completely unknowable or non-extant. Why then, one asks, are there neural correlates of consciousness? Why does there exist a correlation if both mind and matter correlates are mind-projected phenomena? What role does the complex physiology and spatial patterning of the brain play if it is a mere spatiotemporal phenomenon produced by our mind? If the brain were something-in-itself, how could it have causal effects on the mind if causality itself was mere projected phenomena? In general, how could the real world have any effect upon the mind, if causality were not actually real (but merely ideal)? Here we see the polar opposite of emergentism: rather than holding that the brain produces the mind, the mind here produces the brain. Both views rid potency from each side of the correlation.

3:iv – Psycho-Neural Identity Theory

Psycho-neural identity theory (PN-IdT) is that which claims that mental phenomena simply and strictly *are* certain brain activities. An imagined blue triangle simply *is* certain activity in the occipital lobe, for instance. The brain activity does *not cause* the mentality, the mental does *not emerge* from the brain, the mental *is* certain[46] activity in the brain. A number of psycho-neural identity theorists consider emergentism to be a covert dualism,[47] as emergentism accedes to the separation of mind and body considering the relation to be emergence rather than identity (though emergentists themselves tend to identify themselves as materialists).[48]

PN-IdT became prevalent in the mid twentieth century, though it had antecedents in the previous century. I daresay that many today who have not reflected upon the theory endorse it unwittingly. In the philosophy of mind and other disciplines of consciousness, it was rejected wholesale following the publication in the late 1960s and early 70s of a few papers on *multiple realization*: that one mental type could be realized by more than one physical type, thereby voiding the identity of the mental with that physical. To paraphrase Hilary Putnam, if hunger can be realized by both a human and an octopus, it would be incorrect to identify hunger with a merely human type of neurological activity.[49]

An imagined triangle, though it may have neural correlates of consciousness, could not be said to be identical to that neural correlate lest other animals, beings, could not visualize the same triangle. But if we reject emergentism, we can neither say that the triangle emerges from its neural correlates. If we also reject dualism and idealism, where are we left? To delve deeper, let us look at another reason or rejecting PN-IdT: *the spatial property objection*.

It was quickly objected to PN-IdT that if x *is* y, then all the properties (F) of x must also be properties of y. For instance, the morning star has the same properties as the evening star, and thus by Leibniz's Law, or the principle of the identity of indiscernibles – $(x)(y)((F)(Fx \equiv Fy) \supset (x=y))$ – the morning star *is* the evening star (viz. the planet Venus).

Now in the case of the brain and mind, this principle seems to forbid the identity. The properties of spatiality can be used to present this non-identity. But there are, I submit, actually two spatial property objections to PN-IdT rather than the one that was employed in the last century. We can call these two objections the onefold-space property objection and the twofold-space property objection. It is the latter that leads us to hyperspace.

The onefold-space property objection accepts the Cartesian differentiation of matter and mind as a differentiation of the spatial and non-spatial, respectively. If mind is unextended it has properties distinct from extended matter, and as thus cannot be identical. Indeed this is a pivotal argument for Descartes' dualism. If, however, we reject (with James, Smythies, et al.) this Cartesian differentiation, it seems this version of the spatial property objection to PN-IdT no longer holds its power,[50] as both mind and matter have spatial properties. If we reject this Cartesian differentiation, we come then to twofold space, twofold extension. Maintaining twofold space may help PN-IdT to overcome the onefold-space property objection but in its place it threatens PN-IdT with its own twofold-space property objection. Smythies puts the critique thus:

> Two groups of events arranged in a spatial order may not be said to be identical unless they are geometrically congruent. ... [E]vents in the cerebral cortex ... concerned in a particular perception are geometrically non-congruent with the sense-data that these events are alleged, under this [identity] theory, to be. ... [This] can be used to refute with equal finality the theory of psycho-neural identity.[51]

An imagined triangle has its specific spatial properties (angles, boundaries, etc.) which are not identical to the spatial properties of the neuronal activity of which the triangle is the correlate. Therefore by the aforementioned principle of the identity of indiscernibles, the psychological and neurological correlation cannot be a correlation indicating identity.[52]

A mental event then can have (at least) two simultaneous spatial configurations. If we reject dualism, idealism, emergentism, and psycho-neural identity theory, how can we explain this spatial simultaneity? This problem is a specific incidence of the more general mind-matter 'explanatory gap',[53] or 'the hard problem of consciousness'.[54] It is a problem that has proved incendiary and intractable, and requires novel, radical approaches for its solution. One such solution expands the concept of space.

3:v – More-Broad-Smythies Theory

'[It] is impossible that sensa should literally occupy places in scientific space, though it may not, of course, be impossible to construct a space-like whole of more than three dimensions, in which sensa of all kinds, and scientific objects, literally have places. If so, I suppose that Scientific Space would be one kind of section of such a quasi-space, and e.g., a visual field would be another kind of section of the same quasi-space.'[55]

C. D. Broad here proposes that the triangle one imagines and the correlated brain patterns could relate not as identity, duality, emergence, or ideality but as real spaces within a *greater space* that encompasses them both. By 'greater space' is meant one with more dimensions than the three of width, height, and depth – i.e. a space deeper than depth, one that unifies the physical with the mental. Before we explore this theory of mind-matter relation via greater space, let us consider epistemic and ontic possibilities of such space (as illustrated by the hypercube in *Figure 2*, where the top-left-to-bottom-right diagonal represent the fourth dimension of space).

Figure 2

0D	1D	2D	3D	4D
point	line	square	cube	hypercube

Is space not three dimensional by definition? In the fourth century BC, Aristotle asserted so in *On the Heavens*: 'the three dimensions are all that there are',[56] as did Ptolemy in the second century AD.[57] This denial continued through Nicole Oresme, a fourteenth century philosopher and Bishop of Lisieux; Gerolamo Cardano, an Italian algebraist and polymath of the sixteenth century; the Lutheran monk and mathematician Michael Stifel of the same century who writes that a space of more than three dimensions would be 'contrary to nature'[58]; the Jesuit German mathematician and astronomer Christopher Clavius of the sixteenth and seventeenth centuries; and in 1685 the English clergyman and mathematician John Wallis writes that extra dimensionality 'is a Monster in Nature, and less possible than a Chimaera or Centaure. For Length, Breadth and Thick-ness, take up the whole of Space'.[59] This possibility of a space of more than three dimensions, a *hyperspace*, is denied up to modern times, with Hans Reichenbach in 1926 arguing against hyperspace by claiming that it 'would destroy all existing causal laws'[60] (though his speculations on hypothetical hyperspatial phenomenology are phenomenal!).[61]

The first affirmation of the possibility of a fourth spatial dimension comes through the Cambridge Platonist Henry More in his book of 1659, *The Immortality of the Soul*, where he calls the fourth dimension *spissitude*. This rather spiritual apprehension of hyperspace was reflected in the twentieth century by certain writings[62] of the Welsh, Oxford philosopher H. H. Price – who, incidentally, was one of the first philosophers to write on the psychedelic (mescaline) experience.[63] In his later book of 1671, the *Enchiridion Metaphysicum*, More explicitly writes that 'besides the three dimensions which are filled with all extended material things, a fourth must be admitted, with which coincides the spirit'.[64] A century later in 1746, in his very first publication, Immanuel Kant considers hyperspace as the condition of other universes:

> If it is possible that there are extensions of different dimensions, then it is also very probable that God has really produced them

somewhere. For his works have all the greatness and diversity that they can possibly contain. Spaces of this kind could not possibly stand in connection with those of an entirely different nature; hence such spaces would not belong to our world at all, but would constitute their own worlds. I showed above that, in a metaphysical sense, more worlds could exist together, but here is also the condition that, as it seems to me, is the only condition under which it might also be probable that many worlds really exist.[65]

Though Kant is hesitant to concede an actual fourth dimension, he writes concerning its study that, '[a] science of all these possible kinds of space would undoubtedly be the highest geometry that a finite understanding could undertake.'[66]

In 1783, in his later, critical, idealist work, Kant maintained that the threefold dimensionality of space was not something intellectually derivable but something merely based on our human mode of sensing, 'intuition': '[that] space has three dimensions ... cannot at all be shown from concepts, but rests immediately on intuition...'[67]

In Kant's later transcendental idealism, space is not real but a mere human mode of perception through which we frame the real, noumenal, world. Consequently, one can say, the three dimensions of space are but a human projection, not of necessity an actual reality. If space is subjective, then its observed three dimensions cannot be considered a necessarily objective limitation. One of the pioneers of Relativity, the great French mathematician and physicist Henri Poincaré was in agreement:

> [The] characteristic property of space, that of having three dimensions, is only a property of our table of distribution, an internal property of the human intelligence ... . [We] could conceive, living in our world, thinking beings whose table of distribution would be four dimensional and who consequently would think in hyperspace.[68]

It was, arguably, Kant's conjectures that sparked the later interest in the fourth dimension, especially in the later nineteenth century. As one of the most prominent popularizers of hyperspace, the British mathematician Charles Hinton, expressed it in 1888: 'the exploration of the facts of higher [dimensional] space is the practical execution of the great vision of Kant'.[69]

Concurrent to Kant, it must be noted that in 1756, in the famous French *Encyclopédie* edited by Denis Diderot and Jean le Rond d'Alembert, the latter also writes of a fourth dimension, not as spatial but – anticipating Minkowski and Einstein – as temporal:

> One could consider time as a fourth dimension, so that the product of time by volume would, in a certain sense, be the product of four dimensions; this idea is perhaps debatable, but I find it has certain merits…[70]

We will leave to the side the controversial question as to whether time can properly be a dimension of space.[71] But looking back in time, we see that in the shadow of Kant, concepts pertaining to the fourth dimension were being considered in serious fashion by a series of first-rate mathematicians.[72] These mathematicians, first and foremost the German Georg Friedrich Bernhard Riemann, discovered that spaces of any number of dimensions, *n-dimensional space*, were not contradictory or paradoxical, but in fact intelligible and systematically congruent.

Riemann was the student of the equally great mathematician Carl Friedrich Gauss. Gauss had, parallel to János Bolyai and Nikolai Ivanovich Lobachevsky, questioned the soundness of Euclid's fifth postulate, known as the parallel postulate,[73] that had lain unquestioned (as to its truth rather than its proof) for two millennia. Gauss had realized that the fifth postulate was not absolute as it was transgressed through an alternate-yet-valid curved geometry – Euclidean space fell flat in the following way.

Gauss showed that a two-dimensional surface could be determined as being curved in the third dimension through measurements confined to those two dimensions. That is, curvature can be realized internally rather than externally. Let us explain this by poetic analogy.[74] Imagine two-dimensional beings living on the surface of a (three-dimensional) sphere. They cannot ascend to the third dimension and so cannot directly see that what they consider to be a flat plain is in fact curved into an invisible dimension. Gauss showed that even without this extra-dimensional (external) perception, the 2D beings could determine their world's curvature by measuring certain spatial features of their world. For example, they could measure the circumference (c) of a large flat circle and its diameter (d) to find whether the diameter fit 3.14159... (pi, π) times around the circumference. In a flat (0), Euclidean space, $c=\pi d$, as every schoolboy knows. If the two-dimensional beings found this to be precisely the case, then they could rest assured that their world was not curved, just as it appeared to them (so that their perceptions were veridical). If, however, they found that the diameter fit *less* than pi around the circumference – i.e. that the diameter was *longer* than it was supposed to be – this would be indicative of the fact that they lived on a positively curved (elliptic) surface, such as a sphere, in spite of direct perceptions. The diameter of a circle on a sphere would be longer than that on a plane (*Figure 3*). Concisely, if $c = \pi d$, then curvature $(\Delta) = 0$; if $c < \pi d$, then $\Delta > 0$; if $c > \pi d$, then $\Delta < 0$. To make this plain:

Euclidean space   (zero curvature): $(c = \pi d) \supset (\Delta = 0)$ Flat
Elliptic space   (+ve curvature): $(c < \pi d) \supset (\Delta > 0)$ Convex
Hyperbolic space   (-ve curvature): $(c > \pi d) \supset (\Delta < 0)$ Concave

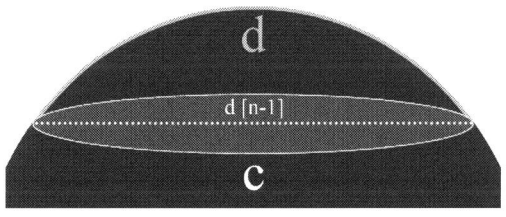

Figure 3

Another method by which to test the curvature of a plain would be to measure the inner angles of a large triangle. If they amounted to 180° then the curvature would be zero, flat. But if they amounted to more than 180°, if there was such an 'angular defect',[75] the measurement would indicate that the surface that appears flat is in fact positively curved, elliptic. A triangle on a sphere bulges, as it were, thus increasing the degree of inner angulation. Conversely, a triangle on a negatively curved surface, such as in a hyperloid, will have inner angles amounting to less than 180°. Euclidean geometry, though three dimensional, concerns flat plains in each dimension where parallel lines never intersect. With the new non-Euclidean, curved geometry of Gauss et al., it was found that this is not the case. For instance, the great circles, orthodromes,[76] of a sphere are parallel lines yet they intersect at the poles.[77]

But non-Euclidean geometry does not *per se* involve more than three dimensions. It was Riemann's imaginative genius that generalized Gauss' method so that these hyperspatial dimensions became intelligible. Instead of limiting the determination of curvature from a (2D) plain to a (3D) space, Riemann developed – in his 1854 paper, 'On the Hypotheses which lie at the Bases of Geometry' – a method by which curvature (n+1) could be determined from any (n) dimensional space. For example, a 3D space can be internally measured to determine curvature in a fourth dimension. In the words of the prominent logical empiricist Hans Reichenbach, '[in] analogy to the auxiliary concept of the curvature of a surface ... Riemann introduced the auxiliary concept of *curvature of space*, which is a much more complicated mathematical structure'.[78] Riemann's ultimate end was to simplify the laws of nature through his complexification of the laws of geometry – for instance by reducing 'force' to curvature.

Euclidean geometry was three dimensional and flat; Gaussian non-Euclidean geometry was three-dimensional and curved; it was Riemannian geometry that allowed for a curved space of more than three dimensions – hyperspace. But the physics of Riemann's age was behind the mathematics, and so his endeavour to explain natural law through geometry was unfulfilled. But his geometry did enable the new physics to come: the theories of Relativity. As physicist and a co-founder of string theory Michio Kaku puts it, 'Einstein fulfilled the program initiated by Riemann 60 years earlier, to use higher dimensions to simplify the laws of nature.'[79] The well-known instance of this is the reduction of the "force" of gravity to spacetime curvature. As we struggle to visualize more than three dimensions, we can explain this through analogy to a lesser dimensionality. Picture our 2D beings approaching a spike that stretches their plane upwards (as we 3D humans see it externally). Though the spike (steep curvature) is imperceptible to the 2D beings, they will nonetheless *feel the curvature* (as "force") as the spike is a stretched space that can entail more effort to traverse. Essentially the distance increases in the imperceptible extra dimension, which requires more effort to pass. As the extra dimension is imperceptible, the curved, extra distance is instead *felt* as a resistant force rather than *seen* as an increased space. If we jump up to our apparent three dimensional world, and add the proviso that matter-energy curves space, the problematic Newtonian mysterious 'action at a distance' is solved not through a mechanical ether but through extra-dimensional geometry. As Bertrand Russell puts it:

> [The] sun exerts no force on the planets whatever. Just as geometry has become physics, so, in a sense, physics has become geometry. The law of gravitation has become the geometrical law that every body pursues the easiest course from place to place, but this course is affected by the hills and valleys that are encountered on the road.[80]

The notion that *imperceptible spatial curvature is perceived through forced feeling rather than vision* is one that was brought out through the English translator of Riemann's aforementioned paper, the great mathematician and philosopher William Kingdon Clifford.[81] In the 1870s Clifford wrote of a hypothetical one-dimensional worm (AB) that lived in a thin oval tube, endlessly circling it clockwise, without any degree of freedom to go counter-clockwise let alone escape 'up' or 'down' (which would be useless concepts to the worm). The worm itself would not even see the second dimension, that is, the oval-like *shape* in which it lives its life. However it would perceive differences in extra-dimensional curvature (i.e. two-dimensional curvature) as *bodily feelings*, because its body would curve more at points of acute curvature (viz. H, E, F, and G in *Figure 4*).[82]

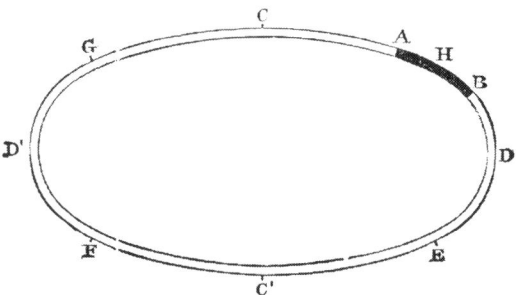

Figure 4: W. K. Clifford's one-dimensional worm

Clifford writes that:

> [A] being existing in these [<3] dimensions would most probably attribute the effects of curvature to changes in its own physical constitution in nowise connected with the geometrical character of its space. ... [If we consider ourselves,] changes in shape may be either imperceptible ... or if they do take place we may attribute them to "physical causes" – to heat, light, or magnetism – which may be mere names for variations in the curvature of our space. ... [We may be] treating merely as physical variations effects which are really due to changes in the curvature of our space; ... some or all of those causes which we term physical may ... be due to the geometrical construction of our space ... variation in the curvature of our space...[83]

Following Einstein's revelations[84] we see how advanced Clifford was, at least with regard to the feeling of gravity. Yet there are perhaps further developments to be made in this field relating extra-dimensional curvature to qualia[85] – thereby correlating not just force to geometry but qualia too. That is to say that a relation of (n-dimensional) space and sentience is here suggested.

Mathematicians and physicists, then, have given feasibility to the idea of n-dimensional space, or hyperspace.[86] We have seen how Clifford relates such space to sentience, let us augment this relation by looking more closely at the ideas of the aforementioned John R. Smythies (1922 – 2019), a neurophilosopher and associate of Aldous Huxley and Humphrey Osmond. Smythies provides two sub-theories through which we can understand the relation of space to sentience:

> *Theory I:* 'Sense-data[87] ... are spatial entities distinct from physical objects and bear temporal and causal relations but no spatial relations to physical objects.'[88] – i.e. an exclusive theory.
>
> *Theory II:* 'Sense data ... are spatial entities distinct from physical objects and bear both temporal and causal relations and higher-dimensional spatial relations to physical objects.'[89] – i.e. an inclusive theory.

Theory I is taken by certain figures such as H. H. Price[90] and Bertrand Russell,[91] but Smythies considers *Theory II* preferable as it is more parsimonious and offers a *contiguous spatial connection* between mind and matter; mind-matter spatial relations that would be lacking in Theory I (which would then only have temporal (i.e. successive) and causal (i.e. transordinal) relations between physical space (PS) and visual space (VS).

Theory I advances that all the three-dimensional spaces of all beings' sense data, and the one three-dimensional space of physicality are a *multiplicity of separate spaces*. In emergentism, each VS would 'emerge' from sections (such as those within brains) of the singular PS.

We have already seen the inadequacy of this mysterious transition.[92] *Theory I* would require causal rather than spatial relations between all myriad spaces, and thus would be an emergentism, and thus the mystery of transordinal nomology emerges once more. Thus we reject *Theory I*.

Theory II then advances the actuality of a *unified space of multiple dimensions* (= *n*-dimensional space) in which all of VS and PS are cross-sections. Moreover, Smythies agrees with psychiatrist Paul Schilder that the *perception* of PS is VS. He quotes Schilder thus: 'The space in which objects are perceived and the space in which they are imaged, are one and the same.'[93] This in turn implies, Smythies writes, that '[in] this *n*-dimensional space Scientific Space [PS] and a visual field [VS] would not be two different *kinds* of section but would merely be two different sections.'[94]

This is not to say that PS is not real but rather to say that our access to it is through VS (plus other senses) which is *prosaically* three-dimensional. Thus the reality of physical space as more than three-dimensional is not falsified by our common perception of it as three-dimensional. I write 'prosaically' because it may be possible to visualize objects of more than three spatial dimensions – Smythies does suggest that '[t]here is no *a priori* reason why we should not develop the ability to appreciate directly an *n*-dimensional spatial system', and there are reports of such vision.[95] *Indirectly*, we can easily conceptualize and work with[96] more than three dimensions of space through algebraic topology using the Cartesian coördinate system where points, areas and volumes, etc., can be located by numeric variables of each dimension's axis, e.g. point h: (x_1, y_2, z_3). To locate a point in a four-dimensional space, one simply adds an axis and its variable, e.g. point h: (x_1, y_2, z_3, w_4). *Ad infinitum*. Alternatively, one can visually *represent* (though not prosaically *present*)[97] four-dimensional space through for instance a four-dimensional cube, or *tesseract* (hypercube) – see *Figure 2*.

The word *tesseract* was coined by the aforementioned mathematician and author Charles Howard Hinton,[98] whose work on the fourth dimension can be used to our ends. In his essay of 1880, 'What is the fourth dimension?' – published four years prior to the related book *Flatland* by Edwin A. Abbott – Hinton employs analogy to lower dimensional worlds to elucidate a speculated four-dimensional world. I shall briefly explain it, then connect this four dimensional world to the *n*-dimensional world of Broad and Smythies, so to entertain a theory of the relation between space and sentience. Note that by four dimensions, we are speaking of four *spatial* dimensions, not a fourth temporal dimension in addition to three spatial dimensions.[99]

Let us imagine a two-dimensional world, a plane, or a *Flatland* as Abbott calls it, like a sheet of paper. Any beings therein would only be aware of two dimensions, and would only be aware of borders describable with two axes (x,y). Thus they would be unaware of the existence (as we perceive it from our three-dimensional perspective) of the top and bottom faces of their plane that is also contiguous, that borders, their two-dimensional world. Now, we three-dimensional observers could see a multiplicity of such planes, sheets, each floating one above the other. Although each entity of the flatland could not perceive the other flatlands (just as in our world *we cannot perceive other entities' experienced three-dimensional spaces*), as they were not contiguous at the x and y axes, *we could* perceive the multitude of flatlands, or worlds, from our higher-dimensional space – and we could perceive the spatial contiguity (i.e. fundamental unity) of two-dimensional worlds in a three-dimensional space. Thus though each such two-dimensional world would not be contiguous with another two-dimensional world,[100] each two-dimensional world would be contiguous with, i.e. *within the same space as*, all the other two-dimensional worlds via the intervening three-dimensional space. Thus the *relationship* between such flatlands would be *spatial rather than merely causal*, under the perspective of a world with a higher dimensionality than that of each two-dimensional world. The nomology would be of one order rather than *transordinal*, because the levels would be unified here. Rather than one world *emerging* from another (as in emergentism), they would each be equally *fundamental and unified*. Now, let me allow Hinton, 1880, to shift the argument up a dimension:

> Take now the case of four dimensions. Instead of bringing before the mind a sheet of paper conceive a solid of three dimensions. If this solid were to become infinite it would fill up the whole of three-dimensional space. But it would not fill up the whole of four-dimensional space. It would be to four-dimensional space what an infinite plane is to three-dimensional space. There could be in four-dimensional space an infinite number of such solids, just as in three-dimensional space there could be an infinite number of infinite planes.
>
> Thus, lying alongside our space, there can be conceived a space also infinite in all three directions. To pass from one to the other a movement has to be made in the fourth dimension, just as to pass from one infinite plane to another a motion has to be made in the third dimension.[101]

Thus we place Smythies' *n*-dimensional spaces (i.e. PS with a multitude of beings' VSs) within the Hintonian four-dimensional space so to render intelligible the *Theory II* relation between VS and PS.

So: through this approach, we exhibit the possibility that though visual spaces and physical space are *not strictly identical*, refuting the Psycho-neural Identity Theory, they *neither need be strictly distinct*, as in Substance Dualism. Neither need one (VS) *emerge* from the other (PS). Through a four-dimensional perspective, we can see that the mental (all of which for James is necessarily spatial)[102] and the physical can be both fundamental and unified, i.e. a mind-matter monism. The imagined triangle and the physical correlates thereof are both part of one n-dimensional space rather than members of distinct categories. This is all to say that the More-Broad-Smythies Theory (*Theory II*) is one, albeit radical, way to respond to the mind-matter mystery. It is a radical monism of space and sentience.

Whether we can call such a monism an identity theory is merely a matter of definition. Spinoza's system, for instance, is certainly a monism and has certainly been classified as an identity theory.[103] In this regard, it is interesting to note that Hinton, in the above-quoted 1880 essay, also writes that:

> In the [four-dimensional manifold] which we have traced out, much that philosophers have written finds adequate representation. Much of Spinoza's *Ethics*, for example, could be symbolized from the preceding pages.[104]

As an example of such representation, consider Spinoza's identity claim that:

> [T]hinking substance and extended substance are one and the same substance, which is comprehended sometimes under the one and sometimes under the other attribute.[105]

It is also interesting to note here that Hinton actually corresponded with William James on the subject of four-dimensional consciousness.[106] Both Spinoza and James were, in the end, panpsychists, and the full extent of the relationship between higher-dimensionality and panpsychism – or more broadly, between n-dimensional space and sentience – is a woefully underexplored world,[107] a world where one may find *idios kosmos* within *koinos kosmos*, thought within extension.

— — —

Notes

1. Diels-Kranz frag. B89.
2. In this chapter I use as synonyms 'mind', 'sentience', 'the mental', and 'experience'.
3. Descartes, 1641/1996, p. 100 (my italics).
4. As Alfred North Whitehead put it: 'The disastrous separation of body and mind which has been fixed on European thought by Descartes is responsible for this blindness of science.' (Whitehead, 1938/1968, p. 154.)
5. James, 1904, pp. 488–489.
6. James, 1879, p. 75.
7. For further analysis of such sentient space and its distinction as such, see Bradley, 1895a; Russell 1948/2009 (pp. 192–7, ch. 6); Smythies, 1958a and 1958b; French, 1987;
8. Russell, 1948/2009, pp. 192 … 196.
9. Whitehead, 1922–3, p. 5.
10. For a good analysis of this distinction and the question concerning the type of space that visual space is, see Rosar, 2016.
11. Merleau-Ponty, 1945/2014, pp. 102–103.
12. James, 1879, p. 75.
13. Merleau-Ponty, 1945/2014, p. 150.
14. Russell, 1925/2009, p. 2.
15. As argued, e.g., by C. A. Strong, 1918, p. 301.
16. In addition to the traditional five senses, I am sympathetic to the additional existence of a primal, causal sense which A. N. Whitehead calls 'perception in the mode of causal efficiency' (see, e.g. Whitehead, 1927/1985, Ch. 2, §4.)
17. James, 1879, p. 70: 'all our sensations, without exception, have this spatial quale.'
18. 'Hyperspace' refers to space of more than three dimensions.
19. This is a term I coined in my article, The Pentalogy of Perception.
20. I do, however, concur with Whitehead's 'organic realism': there is no absolute distinction between an object and its representation (see chapter on the Philosophy of Organism in this volume).
21. '[S]pace which is eternal and indestructible, which provides a position for everything that comes to be, and which is apprehended without the senses by a sort of spurious reasoning and so is hard to believe in – we look at it indeed in a kind of dream …' (*Timaeus*, 52: Plato, c.360BC/1965/1976, p. 70).
22. Lucretius, 2008, p. 15 (Book One, 419–421).
23. See Leibniz's letter V to Samuel Clark, §§29, 62 (Alexander, 1956, pp. 63, 77).

24 https://www.theguardian.com/books/2018/apr/14/carlo-rovelli-exploding-commonsense-notions-order-of-time-interview

25 Rovelli, 2018, p. 77.

26 Ibid., p. 67 (my emphasis).

27 As someone sympathetic to *panpsychism* – the notion that all of physicality includes sentience – I simply note here that if spacetime is a physical object, and if physical objects have sentience, then spacetime itself has sentience. This is distinct from a traditional idealist view that space and time are mere projections of a sentience. The panpsychist can accept the reality of matter, yet imbue it with mind, in a ubiquitous pluralism.

28 This is from a text written in 1676 in Paris, and reproduced in part in Rescher, 1981, p. 90.

29 See the Pentalogy of Perception chapter in this volume for definitions.

30 The neural correlates of consciousness are a subset of the physical correlates of consciousness (see the Panpsychism chapter in this volume).

31 These options are not exhaustive.

32 Smythies, 1994, p. 327.

33 See McLaughlin, 1992.

34 See Broad, 1925, p. 77ff.

35 Note that, in my view, it is not a contradiction to deny free will yet maintain mental causation as a whole. See my doctoral thesis, Chapter 5, §2.

36 For such varieties, see my doctoral thesis, Chapter 5, §2.

37 See Huxley, 1874.

38 Paulsen, 1895, ch. 1, §5, p. 90.

39 Bradley, 1895b.

40 Popper, 1978.

41 See for instance Jaegwon Kim, 2006: '[Emergentists] want to claim that the emergence of consciousness and rational thought has made a fundamental difference to the world at the physical level. It is because of our emergent mental powers that we have built cities and bridges, sent spaceships to Jupiter and Saturn, destroyed rain forests, and burned holes in the ozone layer' (p. 558).

42 See my doctoral thesis, Chapter 2, Part 2.

43 Another problem is that related to the 'causal closure principle' – see e.g. Kim, 2005, Chapter 1.

44 For more against Emergentism, see the chapter on Panpsychism in this volume.

45 See the Transcendental Aesthetetic in Kant, 1781/7/1999.

46 It is not *all* the activity in the brain because much brain activity is not correlated to consciousness.

47 E.g. Smart, 1959, p. 143.
48 See for example Kim, 2005.
49 Putnam, 1967.
50 It should be noted that James considered all types of sensation, not merely the visual and somatic, to be spatial (James, 1879). For a discussion, see my doctoral thesis, Chapter 1, §1:I and Chapter 4, §4-2iii.
51 Smythies, 1956, p. 16.
52 Though note that it could be identity if the 'matter' is an abstraction which in its actual totality can carry more than one spatial configuration. But accepting this view of matter would nonetheless be contrary to the materialism of PN-IdT (see Smart, 1963) and thus would be too much of a qualification to maintain PN-IdT as such.
53 Levine, 1983.
54 Chalmers, 1995. The problem ultimately goes back millennia – the new names merely indicate revived interest.
55 Broad, 1923/1927, pp. 392–3. Note that the inconsistent capitalization of 'scientific space' is as on the original.
56 Aristotle, 1984, p. 447 (228a:9).
57 See Cajori, 1926, p. 397.
58 Ibid., p. 398.
59 Ibid., p. 401.
60 Reichenbach, 1926/1957, p. 274.
61 Ibid., pp. 280–283.
62 Notably Price, 1953.
63 Price, 1963. Price was given mescaline by John R. Smythies (1922–2019 [Jan 28th]), as the latter told me in private correspondence (28 November 2018). Smythies also told me that he gave mescaline to C. D. Broad and R. C. Zaehner.
64 More, 1671, ch. 28, part 1, §7 (via Cajori, 1926).
65 Kant, 1747/2012, p. 28 (§11, I:25).
66 Ibid., p. 28 (§10, I:24).
67 Kant, 1783/1977, pp. 28–9 [Pt. I, §12]).
68 Poincaré, 1906/1913, pp. 177 … 179. In the same text, Poincaré speaks of a type of Japanese mouse that perceives in two dimensions (p. 178).
69 In the essay 'Many Dimensions', 1888, in Hinton, 1896/2008, p. 35.
70 D'Alembert, et al., 1751–1772, p. 4:1010.
71 See for instance Čapek, 1955, and Henri Bergson's works generally.

72   Notably Carl Friedrich Gauss (1777–1855), Nikolai Lobachevsky (1793–1856; 1829: non-Euclidean geometry), János Bolyai (1802–1860; 1832: non-Euclidean geometry), Hermann G, Grassmann (1809–1877; 1844: Extension Theory), Georg F. B. Riemann (1826–1866), William Kingdon Clifford (1845–1879), Charles Howard Hinton (1853–1907), Jules Henri Poincaré (1854–1912), David Hilbert (1862–1943), Hermann Minkowski (1864–1909), and Theodor F. E. Kaluza (1885–1954).

73   The parallel postulate essentially decrees that two parallel lines never intersect.

74   For even more poetic analogy, see the 1844 novel *Flatland: A Romance of Many Dimensions* by A. E. Abbott; the short texts about flat, 2D beings and worlds from the panpsychist and founder of psychophysics, Gustav Fechner (1846 – see Fellner and Lindgren, 2011), those of Charles Hinton (1896/2008), and Evans-Wentz (1911/2016) ch. 11, p. 953: 'It is mathematically possible to conceive fourth-dimensional beings, and if they exist it would be impossible in a third-dimensional plane to see them as they really are. Hence the ordinary apparition is non-real as a form, whereas the beings, which wholly sane and reliable seers claim to see when exercising seership of the highest kind, may be as real to themselves and to the seers as human beings are to us here in the third-dimensional world when we exercise normal vision.'

75   A term coined by Riemann.

76   That is, the largest circles that fit around a sphere, so that their circumferences are identical.

77   Alternating the definition of 'parallel', one could say that parallel lines do not exist in elliptic space.

78   Reichenbach, 1926/1958, p. 10.

79   Kaku, 1994/2016, p. 98.

80   Russell, 1925/2009, p. 80.

81   Clifford was a Cambridge Apostle – see the chapter Concrescence of Dissent in this volume.

82   This is Clifford's own diagram (1885/1904, p. 218).

83   Clifford, 1885/1904, p. 222…223fn…224. Note that Clifford's book is posthumous. He wrote (and dictated) the book in the 1870s (he died in 1879), but it was not published till 1885.

84   As well as the associated four-dimensional Kaluza-Klein theory (1926) that precipitated the n-dimensional String Theories of the 1980s and the M-Theory of the 1990s.

85   'Qualia' means pre-conceptualized experience – such as colours, sounds, scents, feelings, etc. (See Lewis, 1929.)

86   Bernard Carr is a contemporary professor of mathematics and astronomy who has offered his own theories relating n-dimensional space and sentience in line with the More-Broad-Smythies Theory (see, e.g. Carr 2015).

87   By 'sense-data' Smythies refers to visual images.

88 Smythies, 1956, p. 27.
89 Ibid., p. 28.
90 Price, 1953.
91 Russell, 2009/1948.
92 3:ii, above, but also see the chapter on Panpsychism in this volume.
93 Smythies, 1956, p. 47. From Schilder, 1953, p. 41.
94 Smythies, 1956, p. 49.
95 Ibid., p. 124. $n>3$. Though this is in direct contradiction to the seminal figure of hyperspace, mathematician C. H. Hinton who wrote, after years of attempting to achieve such perception, that 'all attempts to visualise a fourth dimension are futile. It must be connected with a time experience in three space' (1904, p. 207). However, fellow hyperspatial mathematician Rudy Rucker claims that in the fifteen years of trying, 'I've enjoyed a grand total of perhaps fifteen minutes' worth of direct vision into four-dimensional space' (Rucker, 1984/6, p. 8). The Dutch orientalist Johan van Manen also writes of experiencing direct vision of four-dimensional space, specifically a four-dimensional globe (1913, pp. 58–61 [Case 15]). There are also reports of psychedelic-induced visions of n-dimensional space. In relation to this, see my review of Andrew Gallimore's book, *Alien Information Theory*.
96 This use was established with Riemann's 1854 thesis, Über *die Hypothesen welche der Geometrie zu Grunde liegen*.
97 Analogously one can represent a 3D cube on a 2D surface (e.g. computer screen), which is not equivalent to seeing a 3D cube as such (due in part to stereopsis).
98 In *The Fourth Dimension*, 1904.
99 To consider time as a fourth spatial dimension, see the thought of Minkowski, 1918, and Ouspensky, 1912/22.
100 If 'two' such worlds met at the x and y axes, this would actually only represent *one* two-dimensional world – just as if we met another world on another planet in our three-dimensional physical world.
101 Hinton, 1880, p. 20.
102 James, 1879, 1904.
103 E.g. Della Rocca, 1993.
104 Hinton, 1884, p. 22.
105 Spinoza, 2018/1677, p. 48 (*Ethics*, II: P7: s).
106 See Throesch, 2017.
107 For an analysis of the relation of hyperspace to analytic metaphysics more generally, see Hudson, 2005/2008.

Chapter Sources

Panpsychism: Ubiquitous Sentience
This chapter is a simplified version of the *Introduction* to my doctoral thesis (Sjöstedt-Hughes, 2019). It was first published online for High Existence magazine on 15 January 2018. It has been modified a little for this book thanks especially to Galen Strawson who provided a final 'peer review' of this chapter.

Conspectus of A. N. Whitehead's Metaphysics
This little summary is a modified transcript of a spoken lecture published online April 13 2015: https://youtu.be/yIj2-lSnQ5M

The Concrescence of Dissent:
Whitehead as Religious, Scientific, Philosophic Heretic
This was the first chapter of the edited volume *Heresy and Borders in the Twentieth Century* (London: Routledge, 2021), pp. 7–27, edited by K. Jakubowicz and R. Dickins. It has been slightly modified.

Psychedelic Experience: Revelation, Hallucination, or Otherwise?
This little essay developed from the talks I gave on the 'Writers on Drugs' tour of 2019 organized by the Psychedelic Press. The essay was commissioned and published online by The Institute of Art and Ideas, the publishing arms of the HowTheLightGetsIn festival, on 12 December 2019.

The Psychedelic Influence on Philosophy
This is a slightly modified version of a very popular text that was commissioned and published online by High Existence on 2 August 2016.

Substance and Process: An Outline
This is a transcript for a lecture I gave to my undergraduate Philosophy of Nature class at The University of Exeter in 2020.

The Great God Pan is Not Dead:
Alfred North Whitehead and the Psychedelic Mode of Perception
This text started out in the form of a presentation I gave at the Interdisciplinary Conference on Psychedelic Research in Amsterdam in 2016. It was a presentation loosely based on my 'Vertexes of Sentience' chapter from my book, *Noumenautics* (Falmouth: Psychedelic Press, 2015), pp. 33–58. I later reworked the talk and published it in the *Psychedelic Press Journal*, issue 20, pp. 47–65 (2017). It is also set to be published in *The Fenris Wolf* journal, issue XII.

The Pentalogy of Perception
This somewhat abstruse text first appeared as an appendix to my doctoral thesis (Sjöstedt-Hughes, 2019). It appears here in slightly modified form.

The First Scientific Psychonaut: Sir Humphry Davy
This text started out as a talk I gave to the Penzance literary Fest and to the Beyond Psychedelics conference in Prague, both in 2018. Thereafter, with help from those acknowledged at the end of the chapter in this book, I published it as an essay in the *Psychedelic Press Journal*, issue 26, pp. 7–32 (2019).

Deeper than Depth: N-Dimensional Space and Sentience

This text appears first here in this book. It is loosely based on a talk I gave at the MIND Foundation in Berlin in April 2019, and subsequently to an audience at the Redwing Gallery in Penzance (Slides: https://youtu.be/Zp2NfDD_isw). It also incorporates a small part of my doctoral thesis.

REFERENCE LIST

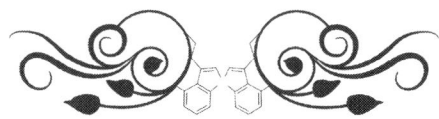

Abbott, A. E. (1844) *Flatland: A Romance of Many Dimensions – by A. Square* (London: Seeley & Co.)

Alexander, H. G., ed. (1956) *The Leibniz-Clarke Correspondence* (Manchester: Manchester University Press)

Alter, T. and Nagasawa, Y. (2012) What is Russellian Monism, *Journal of Consciousness Studies*, 19, pp. 67–95

Ansell-Pearson, K. and Mullarkey, J., eds. (2002) *Henri Bergson: Key Writings* (London: Continuum)

Aristotle (350BC/1984) *On the Heavens*, trans J. L. Stocks, in: *Complete Works of Aristotle, Volume 1*, ed. J. Barnes (Princeton: Princeton University Press), pp. 447–551

Armstrong, D. M. (1989) *Universals: An Opinionated Introduction* (London: Westview Press)

Basile, P. (2017/8) *Whitehead's Metaphysics of Power: Reconstructing Modern Philosophy* (Edinburgh: Edinburgh University Press)

Basile, P. and McHenry, L., eds. (2007) *Consciousness, Reality and Value: Essays in honour of T. L. S. Sprigge* (Frankfurt: Ontos Verlag)

Baudelaire, C. (1860/1996) *Artificial Paradises* (New York: Citadel)

Bayle, P. (1697/1826) *An Historical and Critical Dictionary, Selected and Abridged from the Great Work of Peter Bayle. With a Life of Bayle, in Four Vols.—Vol. III* (London: Hunt and Clarke)

Benjamin, W. (1927–34/2006) *On Hashish* (Cambridge: Belknap Press of Harvard University)

Benjamin, W. (1936/2008) *The Work of Art in the Age of Mechanical Reproduction* (London: Penguin)

Bergson, H. (1896/1999) *Matter and Memory*, 6th edition, trans. N. M. Paul and W. S. Palmer (New York: Zone Books)

Bergson, H. (1907/1998) *Creative Evolution*, trans. A. Mitchell (New York: Dover)

Berkeley, G. (1713/2015) *Three Dialogues between Hylas and Philonous in opposition to Sceptics and Atheists* (New York: Dossier Press)

Bloch, E. (1954–1959/1986) *The Principle of Hope* (Cambridge: MIT Press)

Block, N. (1995) On a Confusion about a function of consciousness, *Behavioral and Brain Sciences*, 18, pp. 227-287

Block, N. (1995) On a Confusion about a function of consciousness, *Behavioral and Brain Sciences*, 18, pp. 227-287

Block, N. and MacDonald, C. (2008) Phenomenal and Access Consciousness: Consciousness and Cognitive Access, *Proceedings of the Aristotelian Society*, New Series, 108, pp. 289–317

Blood, B. P. (1874) *The Anaesthetic Revelation and the Gist of Philosophy* (New York)

Boon, M. (2002) *The Road of Excess: A History of Writers on Drugs* (Cambridge: Harvard University Press)

Bradley, F. H. (1895a) In What Sense are Psychical States Extended?, *Mind*, 4:14, pp. 225-235

Bradley, F. H. (1895b) On the Supposed Uselessness of the Soul, *Mind*, 4:14, pp. 176–179

Broad, C. D. (1923/1927) *Scientific Thought* (London: Kegan Paul, Trench, Trubner & Co.)

Broad, C. D. (1925) *The Mind and Its Place in Nature* (London: Kegan Paul)

Broad, C. D. (1939) 'Arguments for the Existence of God II', *The Journal of Theological Studies*, 40:158

Bruno, G. (1584/1998) *Cause, Principle, and Unity*, eds. R. Blackwell and R. deLucca (Cambridge: Cambridge University Press)

Brüntrup, G. and Jaskolla, L. eds. (2017) *Panpsychism: Contemporary Perspectives* (Oxford: Oxford University Press)

Bucke, R. M. (1901/1947) *Cosmic Consciousness: A Study in the Evolution of the Human Mind*, 13th ed. (New York: E. P. Dutton & Co.)

Cajori, F. (1926) Origins of Fourth Dimension Concepts, *The American Mathematical Monthly*, 33:8, pp. 397–406

Čapek, M. (1955) Relativity and the Status of Space, *The Review of Metaphysics*, 9:2, pp. 169–199

Carhart-Harris, R. L. *et al.* (2016) Psilocybin with psychological support for treatment-resistant depression: an open-label feasibility study, *The Lancet Psychiatry* (published online May 17, 2016 http://dx.doi.org/10.1016/S2215-0366(16)30065-7)

Carpenter, E. (1892) *From Adam's Peak to Elephanta: Sketches in Ceylon and India* (London: Swan Sonnenschein & Co.)

Carr, B. (2015) Hyperspatial Models of Matter and Mind. In: E. F. Kelly, A. Crabtree, and P. Marshall (eds.) *Beyond Physicalism: Toward Reconciliation of Science and Spirituality* (London: Rowman and Littlefield)

Chalmers, D. (1995) Facing Up to the Problem of Consciousness, *Journal of Consciousness Studies*, 2:3, pp. 200–219

Chalmers, D. (1996) *The Conscious Mind: In Search of a Fundamental Theory* (Oxford: Oxford University Press)

Chalmers, D. J. (2016) 'Panpsychism and Panprotopsychism', in: *Panpsychism: Contemporary Perspectives*, eds. G. Bruntrup, G. and L. Jaskolla (Oxford: Oxford University Press), pp. 19–47

Chamovitz, D. (2012) *What a Plant Knows: A Field Guide to the Senses of Your Garden – and Beyond* (London: Oneworld)

Chesterton, G. K. (1925/2006) *The Everlasting Man* (Vancouver: Regent College Publishing)

Clifford, W. K. (1885/1904) *The Common Sense of the Exact Sciences*, 4th ed. (London: Kegan Paul, Trench, Trübner & Co.)

Cobb, J. B. and Griffin, D. R., eds. (1977) *Mind in Nature: the Interface of Science and Philosophy* (Lanham: University Press of America)

Coleridge, S. T. (1817/2014) *Biographia Literaria* (Edinburgh: Edinburgh University Press)

Coleridge, S. T. (1985) *Samuel Taylor Coleridge: The Major Works*, H. J. Jackson, ed. (New York: Oxford University Press)

Collum, B. (1977) *Victorian Country Parsons* (London: Constable and Co.)

Cottingham, J. (1978) "A Brute to the Brutes?": Descartes' Treatment of Animals, *Philosophy*, 53:206, pp. 551–559

Cudworth, R. (1678/1845) *The True Intellectual System of the Universe* (London: Thomas Tegg)

D'Alembert, J.-B. l. R. and Diderot, D. (1751–1772) *Encyclopédie, ou dictionnaire raisonné des sciences, des arts et des métiers*. Online: https://artflsrv03.uchicago.edu/philologic4/encyclopedie1117/navigate/4/4/ [Accessed 27 Sept 2019]

Davy-letters.org.uk [online: accessed 6th July 2018]

Davy, H. (1800) *Researches, Chemical and Philosophical; Chiefly Concerning Nitrous Oxide or Dephlogisticated Nitrous Air, and Its Respiration* (London: Butterworths)

Davy, H. (1830/1889) *Consolations in Travel or The Last Days of a Philosopher* (London: Cassell & Co.)

Davy, H. (1830/2005) *Consolations in Travel; or, The Last Days of a Philosopher* (Circencester: The Echo Library)

De Quincey, T. (1821/1994) *Confessions of an English Opium Eater* (Ware: Wordsworth Editions)

Dean, M and Zamora, M. (2021) *The Last Man Takes LSD: Foucault and the End of Revolution* (New York: Verso)

Deleuze, G. (1969/1990) *The Logic of Sense* (New York: Columbia University Press)

Deleuze, G.and Guattari, F. (1980/2013) *A Thousand Plateaus* (London: Bloomsbury Academic)

Della Rocca, M. (1993) Spinoza's Argument for the Identity Theory, *The Philosophical Review*, 102: 2, pp. 183–213

Descartes, R. (1641/1996) *Discourse on Method and Meditations on First Philosophy*, Weissman, D., ed. (New Haven & London: Yale University Press)

Devereux, P. (1997/2008) *The Long Trip: A Prehistory of Psychedelia* (Brisbane: Daily Grail Publishing)

Donovan, P. (1979) *Interpreting Religious Experience* (London: Sheldon Press)

Eddington, A. S. (1928) *The Nature of the Physical World* (New York: The Macmillan Company)

Edwards, P. (1967) *The Encyclopedia of Philosophy, Vol. VI* (New York: Collier-Macmillan)

Evans-Wentz, W. Y. (1911/2016) *The Fairy-Faith in Celtic Countries* (London: Global Grey)

Farrell, B. A. (1950) Experience, *Mind*, 59:234, pp. 170–198

Fechner, G. T. (1848) *Nanna oder das Seelenleben der Pflanzen* (Leipzig: Leopold Voss)

Fechner, G. T. (1851) *Zend-Avesta, Über die Dinge des Himmels und des Jenseits, vom Standpunkt der Naturbetrachtung* (Leipzig: Leopold Voss)

Fechner, G. T. (1861) *Über die Seelenfrage* (Leipzig: Leopold Voss)

Feigl, H. (1958) 'The "mental" and the "physical"', in: *Minnesota Studies in the Philosophy of Science*, Vol. II, ed. H. Feigl, et al. (Minneapolis: University of Minnesota Press)

Feigl, H. (1967) *The Mental and the Physical: The Essay and a Postscript* (Minnesota: University of Minnesota Press)

Fellner, H. G. and Lindgren, W. F. (2011) Gustav Theodor Fechner: Pioneer of the Fourth Dimension, *The Mathematical Intelligencer*, 33:3, pp. 126–137

Förster-Nietzsche, E. (1915/2007) *The Life of Nietzsche – Volume 2* (London: The Classics)

Foucault, M. (1970) Theatrum Philosophicum, in *Critique*, 282, pp. 885–908 (trans. Donald F. Brouchard and Sherry Simon)

Frege, G. (1918-19/1956) The Thought: A Logical Inquiry, trans. A. M. & M. Quinton, *Mind*, 65:259, pp. 289–311.

French, R. (1987) The Geometry of Visual Space, *Noûs*, 21:2, pp. 115–133

Gallimore, A. (2019) *Alien Information Theory: Psychedelic Drug Technologies and the Cosmic Game* (UK: Strange Worlds Press)

Gerrish, B. A. (1987) The Secret Religion of Germany: Christian Piety and the Pantheism Controversy, *The Journal of Religion*, 67:4 (October), pp. 437–455

Gilbert, A. D. (1980) *The Making of Post-Christian Britain: A History of the Secularization of Modern Society* (London: Longman)

Gilman, S. L., ed. (1987) *Conversations with Nietzsche* (Oxford: Oxford University Press)

Graves, R. (1955/2002) *The Greek Myths*, Vol. 1 (London: The Folio Society)

Green, A., ed. (2016) *"Oh Excellent Air Bag": Under the Influence of Nitrous Oxide, 1799–1920* (Cambridge: PDR Press)

Gregory, T. (2013) 'How Milton Defined Heresy and Why', *Religion & Literature*, 45:1, pp. 148–160

Griffin, D. R. (1998) *Unsnarling the World-Knot: Consciousness, Freedom, and the Mind-Body Problem* (Eugene: Wipf & Stock)

Hartley, H. (1966/1972) *Humphry Davy*, 2nd ed. (Wakefield: EP Publishing)

Hauskeller, C. and Sjöstedt-Hughes, P., eds. (forthcoming 2022) *Philosophy and Psychedelics* (London: Bloomsbury Academic)

Hegel, G. W. F. (1805–6/1892–6/1995) *Lectures on the History of Philosophy, Vol. III: Medieval and Modern Philosophy*, trans. E. S. Haldane and F. H. Simson (Lincoln: University of Nebraska Press)

Heidegger, M. (2004): *Gesamtausgabe IV*. Band 90 *Zu Ernst Jünger* (Frankfurt: Vittorio Klostermannn)

Hinton, C. H. (1880) 'What is the fourth dimension?'. In: R. v. B. Rucker, ed. (1980) *Speculations on the Fourth Dimension: Selected Writings of Charles H. Hinton* (New York: Dover)

Hinton, C. H. (1896/2008) *Scientific Romances, Vol. II* (Leeds: Celephaïs Press)

Hinton, C. H. (1904/2004) *The Fourth Dimension* (Leeds: Celephaïs Press)

Hofmann, A. (1979) *LSD: My Problem Child* (New York: McGraw Hill)

Holmes, R. (2009) *The Age of Wonder: How the Romantic Generation Discovered the Beauty and Terror of Science* (London: Harper Press)

Hudson, H. (2005/2008) *The Metaphysics of Hyperspace* (Oxford: Oxford University Press)

Hume, D. (1739-40/1985) *A Treatise of Human Nature* (London: Penguin)

Huxley, A. (1954/2004) *The Doors of Perception* (Reading: Vintage)

Huxley, T. H. (1874) On the Hypothesis that Animals are Automata, and its History, *The Fortnightly Review*, 16, pp. 555–580

James, W. (1879) The Spatial Quale, *The Journal of Speculative Philosophy*, 13:1, pp. 64–87

James, W. (1882) On Some Hegelisms, *Mind*, 7, pp. 186–208

James, W. (1890/1950) *The Principles of Psychology, Vol. I* (New York: Dover)

James, W. (1902/1985) *The Varieties of Religious Experience* (London: Penguin)

James, W. (1904) Does "Consciousness" Exist?, *Journal of Philosophy, Psychology and Scientific Methods*, 1:18, pp. 477–491

James, W. (1909/1920) *A Pluralistic Universe* (New York: Longmans, Green, and Co.)

James, W. (1910) A Suggestion About Mysticism, *The Journal of Philosophy, Psychology and Scientific Methods*, 7:4, pp. 85–92

Jay, M. (2009) *The Atmosphere of Heaven: The Unnatural Experiments of Dr Beddoes and His Sons of Genius* (New Haven and London: Yale University Press)

Jünger, E. (1920/2004) *Storm of Steel* [*Stahlgewittern*], trans. M. Hofmann (London: Penguin)

Jünger, E. (1970/1980) *Annäherungen: Drogen und Rausch* (Berlin: Klett-Cotta im Ullstein Verlag)

Jünger, E. (1970/2015) *Psykonauterna: Rus och Droge,* trans. S. Jonasson (Umeå: h:ström)

Kaku, M. (1994/2016) *Hyperspace: a Scientific Odyssey through Parallel Universes, Time Warps, and the Tenth Dimension* (Oxford: Oxford University Press)

Kant, I. (1746/2012). Thoughts on the true estimation of living forces and assessment of the demonstrations that Leibniz and other scholars of mechanics have made use of in this controversial subject, together with some prefatory considerations pertaining to the force of bodies in general. In E. Watkins, ed., *Kant: Natural Science (The Cambridge Edition of the Works of Immanuel Kant)* (Cambridge: Cambridge University Press), pp. 1–155

Kant, I. (1766/2002) *Dreams of a Spirit-Seer and Other Writings,* trans. G. R. Johnson and G. A. Magee (West Chester: Swedenborg Foundation)

Kant, I. (1776/2002): *Dreams of a Spirit-Seer [Swedenborg] and Other Writings* (Pennsylvania: Swedenborg Foundation Publishers)

Kant, I. (1781/7/2000) *Critique of Pure Reason*, trans. P. Guyer and A. W. Wood (Cambridge: Cambridge University Press)

Kant, I. (1783/1977) *Prolegomena to Any Future Metaphysics*, trans. P. Carus and J. W. Ellington (Indianapolis: Hackett)

Kant, I. (1784) *An Answer to the Question: "What is Enlightenment?"* (Internet Modern History Sourcebook: Fordham University)

Kant, I. (1788/2002) *The Critique of Practical Reason* (Indianapolis: Hackett)

Keenan, J. F. (1996) Dualism in Medicine, Christian Theology, and the Aging, *Journal of Religion and Health*, 35:1, pp. 33–45

Kim, J. (2005) *Physicalism, or Something Near Enough* (Princeton: Princeton University Press)

Kim, J. (2006) Emergence: Core Ideas and Issues, *Synthese*, 151, pp. 547–559

Kim, J. (2010) *Essays in the Metaphysics of Mind* (Oxford: Oxford University Press)

Kim, J. (2011) *The Philosophy of Mind*, 3rd ed. (Boulder: Westview Press)

Koch, C., Massimini, M., Boly, M., and Tononi, G. (2016) Neural Correlates of consciousness: progress and problems, *Nature Reviews Neuroscience*, 17, pp. 307–321

Koestler, A. (1978) *Janus: A Summing Up* (London: Picador)

Korzybski, A. (1933/1994) *Science and Sanity: An Introduction to Non-Aristotelian Systems and General Semantics*, 5th ed. (New York: Institute of General Semantics)

Kripke, S. (1971) Identity and Necessity. In: M. K. Munitz (ed.) *Identity and Individuation* (New York: New York University Press), pp. 135–64

Kuhn, T. (1962/1970) *The Structure of Scientific Revolutions*, 2nd ed. (Chicago: University of Chicago Press)

Laudan, L. (1981) A Confutation of Convergent Realism, *Philosophy of Science*, 48:1, pp. 19–49

Lefebure, M. (1986) Consolations in Opium: The Expanding Universe of Coleridge, Humphrey [sic] Davy and "The Recluse", *The Wordsworth Circle*, 17:2, pp. 51–60

Lefebure, M. (1990) Humphry Davy: Philosophic Alchemist, in: Gravil and Lefebure, eds. *The Coleridge Connection: Essays for Thomas MacFarland* (New York: Macmillan)

Leibniz, G. W. (1675–1716/1989) *Philosophical Essays*, eds. & trans. R. Ariew and D. Garber (Indianapolis & Cambridge: Hackett)

Levine, J. (1983) Materialism and qualia: the explanatory gap, *Pacific Philosophical Quarterly*, 64, pp. 354–361

Lewin, R. (1980) Is Your Brain Really Necessary? John Lorber, a British neurologist, claims that some patients are more normal than would be inferred from their brain scans, *Science*, 210, pp. 1232–1234

Lewis, C. I. (1929) *Mind and the World-Order: Outline of a Theory of Knowledge* (New York: Dover)

Locke, J. (1690/1964) *An Essay Concerning Human Understanding*, 5th ed. (London: Fontana)

Lowe, V. (1985) *Alfred North Whitehead: The Man and His Work, Volume I* (Baltimore: The Johns Hopkins University Press)

Lowe, V. (1990) *Alfred North Whitehead: The Man and His Work, Volume II* (Baltimore: The Johns Hopkins University Press)

Lucretius (2008) *On the Nature of the Universe*, trans. R. Melville (Oxford: Oxford University Press)

Luke, D. (2013) Ecopsychology and the psychedelic experience, *European Journal of Ecopsychology*, 4, pp. 1–8

Luke, D. (2017) *Otherworlds: Psychedelics and Exceptional Human Experience* (London: Muswell Hill Press)

Lundborg, P. (2012) *Psychedelia: An Ancient Culture, A Modern Way of Life* (Stockholm: Lhasa Mojave)

Machen, A. (1894/2014) *The Great God Pan* (Cathedral Classic—Aziloth Books)

Marcuse, H. (1969) *An Essay on Liberation* (Boston: Beacon Press)

Marincolo, S. (2015) *What Hashish did to Walter Benjamin: Mind-Altering Essays on Marijuana* (Stuttgart: Khargala Press)

McKenna, T. and McKenna, D. (1975/1994) *The Invisible Landscape: Mind, Hallucinogens, and the I Ching,* 2nd ed. (San Francisco: HarperSanFrancisco)

McLaughlin, B. P. (1992) The Rise and Fall of British Emergentism, in: A. Beckermann, H. Flohr and J. Kim, eds., *Emergence or Reduction?: Prospects for Nonreductive Physicalism* (New York: De Gruyter), pp. 49–93

McTaggart, J. M. E. (1908) The Unreality of Time, *Mind,* 17, pp. 457–474

Merleau-Ponty, M. (1945/2014) *Phenomenology of Perception,* trans. D. A. Landes (Abingdon: Routledge)

Michaux, H. (1956/2002) *Miserable Miracle* (New York: New York Review of Books)

Middleton, C. (ed.) (1969/1996) *Selected Letter of Friedrich Nietzsche* (Indianapolis: Hackett)

Minkowski, H. (1918) Time and Space, *The Monist,* 28:2, pp. 288–302

More, H (1671) *Enchiridion Metaphysicum* (London)

More, H. (1659/1987) *The Immortality of the Soul,* ed. A. Jacob (Dordrecht: Martinus Nijhoff Publishers)

Mounce, H. O. (2010) On Dualism, *New Blackfriars,* 91:1034, pp. 401–407

Murray, J. C. (1896) The Idealism of Spinoza, *The Philosophical Review,* 5:5 (September), pp. 473–488

Nagel, E. (1961/1974) *The Structure of Science,* 4th ed. (London: Routledge & Kegan Paul)

Nagel, T. (1974) What is it like to be a bat?, *The Philosophical Review,* 83:4 (October), pp. 435–50

Nagel, T. (1979/2012) *Mortal Questions* (Cambridge: Cambridge University Press)

Nagel, T. (1986) *The View from Nowhere* (Oxford: Oxford University Press)

Neuburg, V. B. (1910/2009) *The Triumph of Pan* (Texas: 100th Monkey Press)

Newton, I. (1704) *Opticks, or a Treatise of the Reflections, Refractions, Inflexions and Colours of Light. Also Two Treatises of the Species and Magnitude of Curvilinear Figures* (London: Smith & Walford)

Nietzsche, F. (1870/1997) The Dionysian Worldview, trans. C. Crawford, *Journal of Nietzsche Studies,* 13, pp. 81–97

Nietzsche, F. (1888/1992) *Ecce Homo,* trans. R. J. Hollingdale (London: Penguin)

Nietzsche, F. (2017) *The Will to Power,* trans. R. Kevin Hill and M. A. Scarpitti (London: Penguin Random House)

Nutt, D., Carhart-Harris, R. L., *et al.* (2012) Neural correlates of the psychedelic state as determined by fMRI studies with psilocybin, in *Proceedings of the National Academy of Sciences,* 109:6, pp. 2138–2143

Nutt, D., Carhart-Harris, R. L., *et al.* (2016) Neural correlates of the LSD experience revealed by multimodal neuroimaging, in *Proceedings of the National Academy of Sciences,* 113:17, pp. 4853–8

Ollard, S. L. and Crosse, G. (1912) *A Dictionary of English Church History* (London: A. R. Mowbray and Co.)

Orage, A. R. (1906) *Friedrich Nietzsche: The Dionysian Spirit of the Age* (London: T. N. Foulis)

Osmond, H. (1957) A Review of the Clinical Effects of Psychotomimetic Agents, *Annals of the New York Academy of Sciences,* 66:3, pp. 418–434

Otto, R. (1923/1958) *The Idea of the Holy* (London: Oxford University Press)

Ouspensky, P. D. (1912/22/2016) *Tertium Organum,* trans. C. Bragdon and N. Bessaraboff (Rookhope: Aziloth Books)

Palmer, W. (1845) *A Compendious Ecclesiastical History from the Earliest Period to the Present Time* [*History of the Church*] (London: James Burns)

Patrizi, F. (1591) *Nova de universis philosophia* (Mamarellus) [Original from the Bavarian State Library. Digitized, 2 March 2012]

Paulsen, F. (1895) *Introduction to Philosophy*, trans. F. Thilly (London: Kegan Paul, Trench, Trubner & Co.)

Paz, O. (1967/1990) *Alternating Current*, trans. H. Lane (New York: Arcade)

Plant, S. (1999) *Writing on Drugs* (London: Faber and Faber)

Plato (1925) *Phaedrus*, in *Plato in Twelve Volumes*, *Vol. 9*, trans. Harold N. Fowler (London: William Heinemann Ltd.)

Plato (1956) *The Works of Plato: the Jowett Translation*, ed. I. Edman, 3rd ed. (New York: Random House)

Plato (1965*) Timaeus and Critias*, 2nd ed., trans. D. Lee (Harmondsworth: Penguin)

Plato (2002) *Five Dialogues: Euthyphro, Apology, Crito, Meno, Phaedo,* 2nd ed. , trans. G. M. A. Grube (Indianapolis: Hackett)

Plato (2003) *The Republic,* trans. D. Lee (London: Penguin)

Plato (2016) *The Laws*, trans. T. Griffith, ed. M. Schofield (Cambridge: Cambridge University Press)

Poincaré, H. (1906/1913) The Relativity of Space, trans. G. B. Halsted, *The Monist*, 23:2, pp. 161–180

Pollan, M. (2018) *How to Change Your Mind: The New Science of Psychedelics* (London: Allen Lane)

Pollock, F. (1880) *Spinoza: His Life and Philosophy* (London: C. Kegan Paul & Co.)

Popper, K. (1978) Natural Selection and the Emergence of Mind, *Dialectica*, 32:3/4, pp. 339–355

Popper, K. R. and Eccles, J. C. (1977) *The Self and Its Brain* (New York: Springer-Verlag)

Price, H. H. (1953) Survival and the idea of 'another world', *Proceedings of the Society for Psychical Research*, 50:182, pp. 1–25

Price, H. H. (1963) A Mescaline Experience, *Journal of the American Society for Psychical Research*, 58:1, pp. 3–20

Price, L. (1954) *Dialogues of Alfred North Whitehead* (London: Max Reinhardt)

Putnam, H. (1967) Psychological Predicates, in: W. H. Capitan and D. D. Merrill, eds., *Art, Mind, and Religion* (Pittsburgh: University of Pittsburgh Press), pp. 37–48

Putnam, H. (1973) *Philosophy and Our Mental Life* (Berkeley: Symposium)

Putnam, H. (1975) *Mind, Language, and Reality: Philosophical Papers*, Vol. 2 (Cambridge: Cambridge University Press)

Reichenbach, H. (1926/1958) *The Philosophy of Space and Time*, trans. M. Reichenbach and J. Freund (New York: Dover)

Rescher, N. (1981) *Leibniz's Metaphysics of Nature* (London: D. Reidel Publishing Co.)

Rescher, N. (1996) *Process Metaphysics: An Introduction to Process Philosophy* (New York: State University of New York Press)

Riemann, B. (1854/2016) *On the Hypotheses Which Lie at the Bases of Geometry*, ed. J. Jost (Basel: Birkhäuser)

Rosar, W. H. (2016) The Dimensionality of Visual Space, *Topoi*, 35, pp. 531–570

Rosenbaum, S. E. (1977) The Property Objection and the Principle of Identity, *Philosophical Studies: An International Journal for Philosophy in the Analytic Tradition*, 32:2, pp. 155–164

Rovelli, C. (2018) *The Order of Time*, trans. E. Segre and S. Carnell (London: Penguin Random House)

Rucker, R. (1984/6) *The Fourth Dimension: and How to Get There* (Harmondsworth: Penguin)

Russell, B. (1911) On the Relations of Universals and Particulars, *Proceedings of the Aristotelian Society*, 12, pp. 1-24

Russell, B. (1912/1980) *The Problems of Philosophy* (Oxford: Oxford University Press)

Russell, B. (1914) Mysticism and Logic, *Hibbert Journal*, 12, pp. 780–803

Russell, B. (1925/2009) *ABC of Relativity* (Abingdon: Routledge)

Russell, B. (1927/2007) *The Analysis of Matter* (Nottingham: Spokesman)

Russell, B. (1940/1969) *An Inquiry Into Meaning and Truth* (London: Pelican)

Russell, B. (1946/2007) *History of Western Philosophy* (London: Routledge)

Russell, B. (1948/2009) *Human Knowledge: Its Scope and Limits* (Abingdon: Routledge)

Russell, B. (1958) *Portraits from Memory and Other Essays* (London: George Allen and Unwin)

Russell, B. (1967/8/9/1991) *Autobiography* (London: Routledge)

Ruston, S. (2013) From "The Life of the Spinosist' to 'Life': Humphry Davy, Chemist and Poet, in: M. Hagen and M. Vibe Skagen, eds. *Literature and Chemistry: Elective Affinities* (Aarhus: Aarhus University Press), pp. 77–97

Sacks, O. (2012) *Hallucinations* (London: Picador)

Santayana, G. (1911) Russell's Philosophical Essays, *The Journal of Philosophy, Psychology and Scientific Methods*, 8:3, pp. 57–63

Santayana, G. (1923/1955) *Scepticism and Animal Faith* (New York: Dover)

Santayana, G. (1927/1940) The Realm of Essence. In: *The Realms of Being* (London: Constable and Co. Ltd.)

Sartre, J-P. (1936/2012) *The Imagination* [*Imagination: A Psychological Critique*] (London: Routledge)

Sartre, J-P. (1938/1965) *Nausea* (London: Penguin)

Sartre, J-P. (1972/1978) *Sartre by Himself* [documentary transcript] (New York: Urizen Books)

Schelling, F. W. J (1800/1997) *System of Transcendental Idealism* (Charlottesville: University Press of Virginia)

Schilder, P. (1953) *Medical Psychology*, trans. Rapaport (New York: International Universities Press)

Schilpp, P. A., ed. (1941) *The Philosophy of Alfred North Whitehead* (Evansyton and Chicago: Northwestern University)

Schopenhauer, A. (1818/1969) *The World as Will and Representation, Volume I*, trans. E. F. J. Payne (New York: Dover)

Schopenhauer, A. (1839/2005) *Essay on the Freedom of the Will* (Mineola: Dover)

Schopenhauer, A. (1844/1966) *The World as Will and Representation, Volume II*, trans. E. F. J. Payne (New York: Dover)

Seager, W. (1995) Consciousness, Information, and Panpsychism, *Journal of Consciousness Studies*, 2:3, pp. 272–288

Sessa, B. (2016) Towards and Integration of Psychopharmacology and Psychotherapy: Using Psychedelic Drug-Assisted Psychotherapy, *Psychedelic Press Journal*, XV, pp. 33–52

Simon, B. and Simon, N. (1972) The Pacifist Turn: An Episode of Mystic Illumination in the Autobiography of Bertrand Russell, *Journal of the American Psychoanalytic Association*, 20:1, pp. 109–21

Sjöstedt-Hughes, P. (2009) Nietzsche and Nihilism, *Ethical Record*, 114:10, pp. 6–10

Sjöstedt-Hughes, P. (2015) *Noumenautics: Metaphysics – Meta-ethics – Psychedelics* (Falmouth: Psychedelic Press)

Sjöstedt-Hughes, P. (2016) The Philosophy of Organism: Whitehead's Organic Awareness of Reality, in: *Philosophy Now*, 114, pp. 22–23 (2016: Anja Publications Ltd). Reprinted in: *The Ultimate Guide to Metaphysics* – from Philosophy Now (2018: Anja Publications Ltd)

Sjöstedt-Hughes, P. (2018) *Conspectus of J. R. Smythies' Theories of Mind, Matter, and N-Dimensional Space*, online: www.academia.edu/37366414/Conspectus_of_J._R._Smythies_Theories_of_Mind_Matter_and_N-Dimensional_Space [accessed 12 June 2019]

Sjöstedt-Hughes, P. (2019) *Pansentient Monism: Formulating Panpsychism as a Genuine Psycho-Physical Identity Theory* (PhD: University of Exeter)

Sjöstedt-Hughes, P. (2019) Why I am not a Physicalist: Four Reasons for Rejecting the Faith, *The Side View*, 1:2, pp. 83–88.

Sjöstedt-Hughes, P. (2022) The White Sun of Substance: Spinozism and the Psychedelic *amor Dei intellectualis*, in: Hauskeller, C. and Sjöstedt-Hughes, P., eds. *Philosophy and Psychedelics: Frameworks for Exceptional Experience* (London: Bloomsbury Academic)

Skrbina, D. (2007) *Panpsychism in the West* (Cambridge: MIT Press)

Smart, J. J. C. (1959) Sensations and brain processes, *The Philosophical Review*, 68:2, pp. 141–156

Smart, J. J. C. (1963) Materialism, *The Journal of Philosophy*, 60:22, pp. 651–662

Smythies, J. R. (1956) *Analysis of Perception* (London: Routledge and Kegan Paul)

Smythies, J. R. (1958a – May) On the Space and Time of Images, *The British Journal for the Philosophy of Science*, 9:33, pp.40–42

Smythies, J. R. (1958b – July) On Some Properties and Relations of Images, *The Philosophical Review*, 67:3, pp. 389–394

Smythies, J. R. (1994) Requiem for the Identity Theory, *Inquiry*, 37:3, pp. 311–329

Spinoza, B. (1670/2001) *Theological-Political Treatise*, 2nd ed., trans S. Shirley (Indianapolis: Hackett)

Spinoza, B. (1677/2001) *Ethics*, trans. W. H. White and A. H. Stirling (Ware: Wordsworth Editions)

Spinoza, B. (1677/2018) *Ethics: Proved in Geometric Order*, trans. M. Silverstone and M. J. Kisner (Cambridge: Cambridge University Press)

Spinoza, B. (1991) *Ethics – Treatise on the Emendation of the Intellect – Selected Letters*, trans. S. Shirley (Indianapolis: Hackett)

Sprigge, T. L. S. (1977) Spinoza's Identity Theory, *Inquiry*, 20, pp. 419–45

Sprigge, T. L. S. (1983) *The Vindication of Absolute Idealism* (Edinburgh: Edinburgh University Press)

Sprigge, T. L. S. (1994) Consciousness, *Synthese*, 98:1, pp. 73–93

Sprigge, T. L. S. and Montefiore, A. (1971) Final Causes, *Proceedings of the Aristotelian Society, Supplementary Volumes*, 45, pp. 149–192

Sprigge, T. L. S. (2006) *The God of Metaphysics* (Oxford: Oxford University Press)

Stamets, P. (2005) *Mycelium Running: How Mushrooms Can Help Save the World* (Berkeley: Ten Speed Press)

Strawson, G. (2013) Real Naturalism, *London Review of Books*, 35:18

Strawson, G. (2018) *Things that Bother Me* (New York: NYRB)

Strawson, G. *et al.* (2006) *Consciousness and its Place in Nature: does Physicalism entail Panpsychism?* (Exeter: Imprint Academic)

Strawson, G., et al.; Freeman, A., ed. (2006) *Consciousness and Its Place in Nature: Does Physicalism entail Panpsychism*? (Exeter: Imprint Academic)

Strong, C. A. (1918) *The Origin of Consciousness: An Attempt to Conceive the Mind as a Product of Evolution* (London: Macmillan and Co.)

Symons, A. (2015) *Aldous Huxley's Hands: His Quest for Perception and the Origin and Return of Psychedelic Science* (New York: Prometheus Books)

Throesch, E. L. (2017) Four-dimensional consciousness: the correspondence between William James and Charles Howard Hinton, in: *Before Einstein: The Fourth Dimension in Fin-de-Siècle Literature and Culture* (London: Anthem Press), pp. 284–349

Tylor, E. B. (1871) *Primitive Culture: Researches in to the Development of Mythology, Philosophy, Religion, Art and Custom*, Vol. I (London: John Murray)

Van Manen, J. (1913) *Some Occult Experiences* (Chicago: Theosophical Publishing House)

Viereck, G. S. (1930) *Glimpses of the Great* (New York: The Macauley Company)

Volney, C. F. (1796/1869) *Volney's Ruins: or, Meditation on the Revolutions of Empires*, trans. Count Daru (Boston: Josiah P. Mendum)

Waddington, C. H. (1961) *The Nature of Life* (London: George Allen & Unwin Ltd)

Wang, H. (1987) *Reflections on Kurt Gödel* (Cambridge: the MIT Press)

Wasson, R. G., Hofmann, A., Ruck, C. A. P. (1978/2008) *The Road to Eleusis: Unveiling the Secrets of the Mysteries* (Berkeley: North Atlantic Books)

Waterfield, R. (2000/2009) *The First Philosophers: The Presocratics and the Sophists* (Oxford: Oxford University Press)

Watts, A. (1962/2013) *The Joyous Cosmology: Adventures in the Chemistry of Consciousness* (Novato: New World Library)

Watts, A. (1966/2011) *The Book on the Taboo Against Knowing Who You Are* (London: Souvenir Press)

Watts, A. (1968) Psychedelics and Religious Experience, *California Law Review*, 56:1, (January), pp. 74–85

Wells, H. G. (1895) *The Time Machine* (London: William Heinemann)

Whitehead (1938/58) *Modes of Thought* (New York: Capricorn Books)

Whitehead, A. N. (1898/2009) *A Treatise on Universal Algebra* (Cambridge: Cambridge University Press)

Whitehead, A. N. (1919) *An Enquiry Concerning the Principles of Knowledge* (Cambridge: Cambridge University Press)

Whitehead, A. N. (1920/2004) *The Concept of Nature* (New York: Prometheus Books)

Whitehead, A. N. (1922–3) Uniformity and Contingency: The Presidential Address, *Proceedings of the Aristotelian Society*, New Series, 23, pp. 1–18

Whitehead, A. N. (1925/1997) *Science and the Modern World* (New York: The Free Press)

Whitehead, A. N. (1926/2011) *Religion in the Making* (New York: Cambridge University Press)

Whitehead, A. N. (1927) *Symbolism: Its Meaning and Effect* (New York: Macmillan Co.)

Whitehead, A. N. (1927/1985) *Symbolism: Its Meaning and Effect* (New York: Fordham University Press)

Whitehead, A. N. (1927/2011) *Religion in the Making* (Cambridge: Cambridge University Press)

Whitehead, A. N. (1929) *The Function of Reason* (Princeton: Princeton University Press)

Whitehead, A. N. (1929/1985) *Process and Reality: An Essay in Cosmology*, corrected ed. (New York: Free Press)

Whitehead, A. N. (1933/1967) *Adventures of Ideas* (New York: The Free Press)

Whitehead, A. N. (1938/1958) *Modes of Thought* (New York: Capricorn Books)

Whitehead, A. N. (1938/1968) *Modes of Thought* (New York: The Free Press)

Whitehead, A. N. (1941) 'Autobiographical Notes', in: P. A. Schilpp, ed. *The Philosophy of Alfred North Whitehead* (Evansyton and Chicago: Northwestern University), pp. 3–14

Whitehead, A. N. (1961) *The Interpretation of Science: Selected Essays*, ed. A. H. Johnson (New York: Bobbs-Merrill Co.)

Whitehead, A. N. (n.d.) Religious Psychology of the Western Peoples, ADD020, Whitehead Research Library: http://wrl.whiteheadresearch.org/items/show/1414

Wordsworth, W. (1994) *The Works of William Wordsworth* (Ware: Wordsworth Editions)

Zaehner, R. C. (1957) *Mysticism Sacred and Profane* (New York: Oxford University Press)

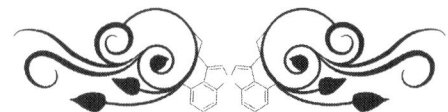

Philosopher of mind **Dr Peter Sjöstedt-Hughes** is a research fellow and associate lecturer at the University of Exeter. Peter is the author of *Noumenautics*, the TEDx Talker on 'Psychedelics and Consciousness', and he is inspiration to the inhuman philosopher Marvel superhero, Karnak.

www.philosopher.eu

Printed in Great Britain
by Amazon

74400875R00132